How Does Violent Media Affect Youth?

Bonnie Szumski and Jill Karson

INCONTROVERSY

ReferencePoint
Press®

San Diego, CA

About the Author

Bonnie Szumski has been an editor and author of nonfiction books for twenty-five years. Jill Karson has been an editor and author of nonfiction books for young adults for fifteen years.

© 2014 ReferencePoint Press, Inc.
Printed in the United States

For more information, contact:
ReferencePoint Press, Inc.
PO Box 27779
San Diego, CA 92198
www. ReferencePointPress.com

Picture credits:
Cover: iStockphoto.com
AP Images: 46
© Mike Blake/Reuters/Corbis: 72
© Andrew Burton/Reuters/Corbis: 9
© Julio Cortez/AP/Corbis: 66
© Ewing Galloway/ClassicStock/Corbis: 20
© Chris Keane/Reuters/Corbis: 50
© Justin Lane/epa/Corbis: 57
Photofest Images: 16, 32, 70, 78
© Paul Sakuma/AP/Corbis: 39
Thinkstock Images: 24

LIBRARY OF CONGRESS CATALOGING-IN-PUBLICATION DATA

Szumski, Bonnie, 1958–
    How does violent media affect youth? / by Bonnie Szumski and Jill Karson.
      p. cm. -- (In controversy series)
    Includes bibliographical references and index.
    ISBN 978-1-60152-616-8 (hardback) -- ISBN 1-60152-616-4 (hardback)
  1. Mass media and youth. 2. Youth and violence. 3. Aggressiveness in adolescence. 4. Violence in mass media. I. Karson, Jill. II. Title.
    HQ799.2.M35S98   2014
    303.60835--dc23
                                                                        2013031021

Contents

Foreword

I n 2008, as the US economy and economies worldwide were falling into the worst recession since the Great Depression, most Americans had difficulty comprehending the complexity, magnitude, and scope of what was happening. As is often the case with a complex, controversial issue such as this historic global economic recession, looking at the problem as a whole can be overwhelming and often does not lead to understanding. One way to better comprehend such a large issue or event is to break it into smaller parts. The intricacies of global economic recession may be difficult to understand, but one can gain insight by instead beginning with an individual contributing factor, such as the real estate market. When examined through a narrower lens, complex issues become clearer and easier to evaluate.

This is the idea behind ReferencePoint Press's *In Controversy* series. The series examines the complex, controversial issues of the day by breaking them into smaller pieces. Rather than looking at the stem cell research debate as a whole, a title would examine an important aspect of the debate such as *Is Stem Cell Research Necessary?* or *Is Embryonic Stem Cell Research Ethical?* By studying the central issues of the debate individually, researchers gain a more solid and focused understanding of the topic as a whole.

Each book in the series provides a clear, insightful discussion of the issues, integrating facts and a variety of contrasting opinions for a solid, balanced perspective. Personal accounts and direct quotes from academic and professional experts, advocacy groups, politicians, and others enhance the narrative. Sidebars add depth to the discussion by expanding on important ideas and events. For quick reference, a list of key facts concludes every chapter. Source notes, an annotated organizations list, bibliography, and index provide student researchers with additional tools for papers and class discussion.

The *In Controversy* series also challenges students to think critically about issues, to improve their problem-solving skills, and to sharpen their ability to form educated opinions. As President Barack Obama stated in a March 2009 speech, success in the twenty-first century will not be measurable merely by students' ability to "fill in a bubble on a test but whether they possess 21st century skills like problem-solving and critical thinking and entrepreneurship and creativity." Those who possess these skills will have a strong foundation for whatever lies ahead.

No one can know for certain what sort of world awaits today's students. What we can assume, however, is that those who are inquisitive about a wide range of issues; open-minded to divergent views; aware of bias and opinion; and able to reason, reflect, and reconsider will be best prepared for the future. As the international development organization Oxfam notes, "Today's young people will grow up to be the citizens of the future: but what that future holds for them is uncertain. We can be quite confident, however, that they will be faced with decisions about a wide range of issues on which people have differing, contradictory views. If they are to develop as global citizens all young people should have the opportunity to engage with these controversial issues."

In Controversy helps today's students better prepare for tomorrow. An understanding of the complex issues that drive our world and the ability to think critically about them are essential components of contributing, competing, and succeeding in the twenty-first century.

Media Violence Versus Real Violence

Numerous studies have attempted to prove that media violence is responsible for real violence—especially in connection with recent mass shootings. These studies, so far, have not proved a link exists. The assertion of such a link, however, is one of the most highly discussed in the debate on the topic.

Many contend that the assertion that media violence has a hand in real-life violence is the same as the age-old argument about what came first, the chicken or the egg. Do viewing violence and/or playing violent video games propel someone to commit violent acts? Or are certain people more vulnerable than others and more prone to violence, and thus more attracted to media such as violent video games, in which they can act it out?

Clearly Troubled

Several of the more recent mass shootings are certainly examples of troubled, mentally ill men, some of whom also played violent video games. Adam Lanza is one example. On December 14, 2012, twenty-year-old Lanza fatally shot twenty children and six adult staff members in a mass murder at Sandy Hook Elementary School in the village of Sandy Hook in Newtown, Connecticut. He also shot and killed his mother in the home that the two shared. Lanza had a long history of mental problems, which his mother had attributed to his Asperger's syndrome, a mild form of autism.

When police entered Lanza's home after the shootings, they found a basement lair filled with weapons, thousands of dollars' worth of violent, shooting-type video games, and collections of articles about other mass shootings. Lanza was obsessed with guns, an obsession his mother indulged by taking him to shooting ranges on outings, buying guns, and allowing Lanza to play video games for hours.

Lanza is not alone. Anders Breivik shot sixty-nine people, mostly teenagers, in a 2011 attack in Norway. James Holmes shot and killed twelve people and injured fifty-eight in 2012 in a theater in Aurora, Colorado. Police say Holmes would have killed more if his magazine had not stuck, preventing him from continuing to shoot. All of these shooters exhibited signs of mental illness, all were avid video gamers, and all ended up being perpetrators of mass shootings. In the case of Holmes, he chose a theater playing the Batman film *The Dark Knight Rises* because he claimed to be the Joker, of whom Batman's butler Alfred remarked: "Some men just want to watch the world burn."[1] New stories after each event were filled with anguished articles about how to stop these incidents. One persistent argument was to ban or regulate violent video games to prevent such carnage, in spite of the fact that no causal relationship between video game play and violence had been proved.

> "Nobody can sit here for certain and say that without any one of those things, without the powerful weapons, without the mental illness, without the exposure to video games, this wouldn't have happened. . . . But we do see a trend where some of these shooters do have exposure to these video games."[2]
>
> — Connecticut senator Chris Murphy, commenting on Adam Lanza's shooting rampage.

What Can Be Done?

Some argue that these incidents alone are enough to warrant censoring violent video games. Connecticut senator Chris Murphy agrees with this view: "Now, nobody can sit here for certain and say that without any one of those things, without the powerful weapons, without the mental illness, without the exposure to video games, this wouldn't have happened. We can't put ourselves in his [Lanza's] mind. But we do see a trend where some of these shooters do have exposure to these video games."[2]

Others believe that the focus should be on isolating and tracking people with mental illness, especially making sure that the mentally ill are incapable of purchasing weapons, though no one is sure exactly how this would be carried out. In the United States, such tracking would violate First Amendment rights. *Slate* reporter William Saletan argues that the carnage mandates that something be done to track the mentally ill and prevent them from obtaining guns and ammunition:

> When I look at all the documents, the common thread is mental illness. Worries and warnings about it weren't heeded or shared . . . Holmes merited an alert to a college threat assessment team, but not to the dealers who sold him 6,000 rounds. Lanza's mother, lost in denial, failed to recognize that he shouldn't be anywhere near a firearm.
>
> Disclosing mental health problems makes all of us uneasy. We don't want to live in a country where every therapy session is public information. Many of us don't want to live in a country where guns are confiscated over gossip. I can't tell you how to link weapon sales to behavioral assessment in a way that avoids those scenarios. But I can tell you this: Until we do, there will be more carnage.[3]

The mother of one mentally ill son in his twenties, Dottie Pacharis, talks of how he believed he was hunted by the government and had several times threatened others with violence. She agrees that mental illness is the problem. But instead of relating it to gun buying, she makes a plea for more help for mentally ill adults. Once a child becomes an adult, a parent can no longer interfere in his or her treatment, make sure he or she complies with taking medication, nor make a mandatory commitment if the situation becomes dire. It was not until her son assaulted a police officer that Pacharis managed, by petitioning the court, to get him committed to a psychiatric hospital instead of being sent to prison. Under the care of psychiatrists and with mandatory compliance with medications, her son's condition quickly improved. But once released, he went off his meds again and quickly became delusional—and there was little the family could do. She explains:

When he stopped taking his meds, both he and his family suffered the consequences. During a manic episode, he lost touch with reality and lacked the ability to recognize he was ill. Families are—or can be—the early warning system. They see the fuse burning long before the bomb goes off, but there is nothing concerned families can do until their loved one reaches the crisis stage. . . .

When he told me of his plan to bear arms to protect himself from federal agents he felt certain were trying to assassinate him, I feared he might actually purchase a gun and shoot innocent victims he mistook for federal agents. I called the FBI to confirm his name was in the database used by licensed firearm dealers to run background checks on prospective buyers. Because of the privacy laws, I was unable to confirm my son's name was in that database.[4]

Mourners light candles at a memorial for the children and adults killed in a shooting at Sandy Hook Elementary School in Connecticut in 2012. Several recent mass shootings, including this one, were committed by troubled young men who had a history of playing violent video games.

A Complicated Issue

Pacharis believes that preventing people with mental illness from obtaining guns is not the answer. Instead, parents, school psychologists, and others who are the first to notice such issues should be allowed to contact the authorities and have such individuals evaluated by competent mental health professionals.

In the United States, however, people with mental illness have civil rights just like any other citizen. No matter how delusional, they have privacy rights, for example, that prevent someone from gathering mental health records from another state without the patient's consent. This allows patients to move from state to state without authorities understanding the seriousness of their condition. In addition, privacy laws make it difficult for parents to have a say in an adult child's visits with a psychiatrist. In the cases of Lanza and Holmes, for example, parents and counselors both tried to help them but could not do so without consent, allowing both to fall even deeper into a psychotic state.

Yet the mentally ill themselves fear such state powers. Those that are on their medications and have their illnesses under control feel especially vulnerable when such discussions take place. Freelance writer Dennis Scimeca, who has bipolar disorder and a plays a number of violent video games, contends:

> "What might have made me a school shooter in some other reality would have been whether I was lonely, or whether anyone was paying any attention to the fact that I was in constant pain, or whether I could have easily laid my hands on a lot of guns, and I'm very glad that in my case none of those things were true."[6]
>
> — Dennis Scimeca, a freelance writer and video gamer with bipolar disorder.

People speculate that violent games and mental illness mix badly. They theorize that the former exacerbates the latter.

I can't listen to conversations about mental illness and violent video games—all the speculation that those games could inspire the mentally ill to commit these atrocities—and not think that these people are also talking about me.

I hear those conversations at work or in mixed company. Sometimes I hear them from the mouths of family members when they visit and see me playing Halo 4 or Battlefield 3.

I quietly listen to the speculation and the concern and don't say a word, even though I want to say, "I'm mentally ill, I've gorged on violent video games my entire life, and they've never made me feel like doing harm to another human being.[5]

Scimeca is just as appalled by the recent shootings as any other person. He does concede that other factors, however, may have allowed him to act out on his sometimes violent revenge fantasies against his schoolmates' constant teasing and bullying: "What might have made me a school shooter in some other reality would have been whether I was lonely, or whether anyone was paying any attention to the fact that I was in constant pain, or whether I could have easily laid my hands on a lot of guns, and I'm very glad that in my case none of those things were true."[6] Studies show that it takes more than exposure to media violence to cause someone to engage in a mass shooting on the scale of an Adam Lanza or James Holmes. What changes are needed to prevent such tragedies will remain part of the discussion.

What Are the Origins of the Media Violence Debate?

In the debate over media violence, three issues predominate. The first is that media violence spawns imitative behavior—the idea that watching violence in the media causes a person to act out in a similar way. The second is that watching media violence desensitizes the viewer into tolerating more violence in the real world. The last idea is that watching media violence causes people to become more unrealistically fearful of the real world. Of these three ideas, the first is the most persistent and has been the subject of the most regulation and research. Lawmakers and others argue that the more explicit and gory violence has become—in television, in video games, and in movies—the worse violent crime has become. However, some critics argue that violence in media is not a recent phenomenon and cannot be blamed for increased violence in everyday life. Violence—in art, literature, and spectacle—is part of the fabric of what makes a good story and has been around as long as civilization. Media scholar Henry Jenkins comments:

> Why is violence so persistent in our popular culture? Because violence has been persistent as a theme across storytelling media of all kinds. A thorough account of violence

12

in media would include: fairy tales such as Hansel and Gretel, oral epics such as Homer's *The Illiad*, the staged violence of Shakespeare's plays, fine art paintings of the Rape of the Sabine Women, and stain glass window representations of Saints being crucified or pumped full of arrows, or for that matter, talk show conversations about the causes of school shootings. If we were to start going after media violence, then, we would need to throw out much of the literary cannon and close down all of our art museums. Violence is fundamental to these various media because aggression and conflict is a core aspect of human experience. We need our art to help us make sense of the senselessness of violence in the real world, to provide some moral order, to help us sort through our feelings, to provoke us to move beyond easy answers and ask hard questions.[7]

A Long History of Concern About Media Influences

While Jenkins's point seems sound, critics today would argue that comparing today's violent media with literary history is not an apt comparison. Media has moved beyond books and performances of plays to nearly every format of communication and entertainment available in modern life. And as media has become more varied—including dime novels, comic books, movies, music, computer games, television, and the Internet—it has become more controversial for its effects on youth. However, this theme is also not a new one. In the nineteenth century, for example, the novel was considered a particularly bad influence on people because its subject matter was violent. Many popular novels of the day described in lurid detail settlers being captured, tortured, and killed by Native Americans. Other popular genres included graphic descriptions of seduction, rape, and other forms of violence. Many thought this material threatened mental health and the very fabric of society. Clearly, novels did not disrupt civilization nor spawn imitations.

Newspapers, too, were condemned as appealing to people's more prurient side, using violent and often misguided headlines and lurid descriptions of crimes to draw a larger audience. Dur-

An Overly Broad Definition of Media Violence

Many media scholars insist that though media violence continues to be avidly studied, the findings are overly broad. According to Tom Grimes, professor of mass communication and adjunct research professor at Texas State University:

> Beginning in the 1970s, researchers began defining media violence so broadly that it lost its meaning. Violence was defined as anything ranging from the content of children's cartoons to the realistic portrayals of violence in movies. The absurdity of this definition shows up in the often repeated claim that by the time a child finishes elementary school, that child has seen 8,000 murders and 100,000 other acts of violence on TV.
>
> Consider what this means. Dramatically or comically portrayed violence is elevated to the same order of magnitude as witnessing real violence on TV. Does that make sense? The difference between fictional violence and real violence gets at the very meaning of what "violence" is and what puts people on their guard vs. what entertains them.
>
> Researchers have expanded the definition of aggressive behavior, as well. They have defined it as "any aggressive act against another person"—giving the middle finger to other people, accumulating a lot of traffic violations, verbal expressions of materialism, admissions of making mean faces at others, and criticizing the appearance of others. Based on those definitions, the American population is a seething mob of miscreants.

Tom Grimes, "Define Violence in the Media: Column," *USA Today*, January 20, 2013. www.usatoday.com.

ing the late 1890s, for example, when a battle between newspaper owners Joseph Pulitzer II and William Randolph Hearst brought about a tide of "yellow journalism," defined as sacrificing truth to draw readers in to sensational stories, newspaper headlines were particularly vivid. Such stories appealed to many readers, resulting in an uptick in sales. The link between people's thirst for such media and the possible harms that might result from that exposure became a theme that continues today.

Any media that discussed the dark side of humanity was open to public condemnation. In the 1940s and 1950s comic books were singled out for attack. As media scholar Steven J. Kirsh describes:

> Comics were thought to weaken the use of good manners, teach lawlessness, cheapen life, and increase the chance of mental illness. . . . Comic books depicted burlesque, slapstick humor, crime, adventure, and, of course, superheroes. Although concern was raised over the tawdry nature of comic book characters, the glorification of violence as a means of problem solving, and the promotion of gay (e.g., Batman and Robin) and lesbian (e.g., Wonder Woman) lifestyles, it was the "Crime Comics" that were most often viewed as evil influences by society. . . . Brandishing titles such as Gangsters and Gun Molls, Crimes by Women, and March of Crime, the story lines of crime comics involved stealing, murder, mayhem, torture, and other criminal activities. In the 1940s, nearly 50 cities attempted to ban the sale of crime comics.[8]

Throughout the 1950s individual cities were under such pressure to regulate comic book content that some, such as Oklahoma City, Oklahoma, and Houston, Texas, passed ordinances that banned crime and horror comics. Some cities organized public burnings of comic books. In response to public concern, the Senate Subcommittee on Juvenile Delinquency commenced hearings on the topic of violent content in comic books. The hearings led to the creation of the Comics Code Authority (CCA) in 1954, a body of people that rated comic books based on a rating system. The code banned graphic depictions of violence and gore in crime

Batman and other comic book characters were condemned in the 1940s and 1950s as a vehicle for glorifying violence and influencing evil behavior. Pictured is a 1954 Batman comic book cover.

and horror comics. It also banned sexual content and innuendo. Comic book publishers submitted the books to the CCA. If the content was found acceptable under the rating system, the publisher was allowed to use the CCA's seal of approval. Although the CCA had no official control over publishers, many complied with the rating system because many sellers of comics refused to sell them without the seal. The CCA slowly died away as more and more publishers refused to comply with it.

Movies and Morals

While fears of print media were widespread, it was the advent of motion pictures in the early 1900s that led to renewed fears of children's exposure to violence. Newspaper editorials denounced films for harming the morals of children. As Kirsh describes: "Movie theaters were viewed as training grounds for criminals, offering children opportunities to watch acts of degradation and learn 'values' not taught in Church or at home. Anecdotal evidence of the evil influence of motion pictures was reported in newspapers; mothers complained that films caused their sons to run away from home, steal money, or learn the art of burglary."[9]

The fear of movies' influence on behavior led to one of the first empirical research studies on media violence. The research firm, the Payne Fund, sponsored a series of studies in the 1930s to investigate the effect of movies on children. Although the studies could not provide a causal link between violent behavior and movies, the authors argued that some boys and young men "when suitably predisposed, sometimes have utilized techniques of crime seen in the movies" or "idealized themselves imaginatively as possessing as attractive a personality, or as engaging in as romantic activities as gangster screen heroes."[10]

While such studies were inconclusive, the public still believed that the movie industry had to respond. As with the CCA, such concerns led to the implementation of a rating system for films. In 1922 film companies formed an organization called the Motion Picture Producers and Distributors of America (MPPDA) to help rate and regulate films. The MPPDA was led by Will Hays, and its production code, adopted in 1930, was often called the Hays Code after him. Though the code had no legal power to limit films, it was universally adopted because many movie houses refused to show films that did not carry a rating. The code's general principles held that

"Movie theaters were viewed as training grounds for criminals, offering children opportunities to watch acts of degradation and learn 'values' not taught in Church or at home."[9]

— Author and media scholar Steven J. Kirsh.

1. No picture shall be produced that will lower the moral standards of those who see it. Hence the sympathy of the audience should never be thrown to the side of crime, wrongdoing, evil or sin.

2. Correct standards of life, subject only to the requirements of drama and entertainment, shall be presented.

3. Law, natural or human, shall not be ridiculed, nor shall sympathy be created for its violation.[11]

These particular principles were the code's focus because it was thought that youth were vulnerable to the influence of films and would copy the behavior they saw in them. Not surprisingly, having been written by religious leaders, the Hays Code had distinct religious language and warned that art could be "morally evil in its effects." The code was especially concerned that "the audience feels sure that evil is wrong and good is right."[12] Though the code was modified several times until it was replaced in 1968 by a version of the rating code that is in force today, it effectively censored American-made films for decades.

Television Brings New Fears

New technologies led to new fears. Introduced in the 1940s, television quickly made entry into people's homes, and its easy access led many to fear its influence. By 1960 the number of television sets in the United States had surpassed the number of homes. The overwhelming popularity of television led to concern about the effects of television on children. Although Congress held its first hearing on the subject in 1952, it did not feel the need to take immediate action. The National Association of Radio and Television Broadcasters, fearing such interference, had already adopted a code to regulate broadcast content. In 1954 and 1955, however, the Senate held hearings on juvenile delinquency and television. As with previous codes for radio and movies, the Senate wanted a code that governed the depiction of topics such as crime, sex, and law enforcement. The Senate report outlined a code for television and detailed the mechanism by which the code was to be enforced.

The Hays Code

The Hays Code that governed the production of most American movies from 1930 to the late 1960s stipulated the following prohibitions against the portrayal of crime and violence:

1. Murder
   a. The technique of murder must be presented in a way that will not inspire imitation.
   b. Brutal killings are not to be presented in detail.
   c. Revenge in modern times shall not be justified.
2. Methods of Crime should not be explicitly presented.
   a. Theft, robbery, safe-cracking, and dynamiting of trains, mines, buildings, etc., should not be detailed in method.
   b. Arson must be subject to the same safeguards.
   c. The use of firearms should be restricted to the essentials.
   d. Methods of smuggling should not be presented.
3. Illegal drug traffic must never be presented.

The Motion Picture Production Code, "The Production Code of the Motion Picture Industry." http://productioncode.dhwritings.com.

Rules that applied to television were more stringent than those that applied to film; they included restrictions on showing a married couple in the same bed and depictions of a crime, greed, or avarice.

Television's effects on children's behavior were tested with empirical research. In the 1960s researcher Albert Bandura conducted a series of experiments using children, adults, and a "Bobo" doll, an inflatable, pear-shaped rubber doll with a weighted bottom that bounced back when hit or punched. Forty-eight girls and forty-eight boys were divided into three experimental groups and one control group. Group 1 watched an adult punch the Bobo doll and call it names. Group 2 watched a film of the adult punching and calling the Bobo doll names, while Group 3 watched a cartoon of a cat punching the Bobo doll. (The control group played with other toys.) After the viewings, all of the groups of children were exposed to a frustrating situation in order to heighten their aggression. Next, the children were allowed to play in a room full of toys that also included the Bobo doll and various implements

A couple shops for a new television in the 1960s. As television became increasingly popular, concerns about the effects of television on children also grew.

to hit the doll. Bandura's results showed that the children who had been exposed to the aggressive behavior, whether real-life, on film, or cartoon, were nearly twice as aggressive as the control group. It was also found that boys exhibited more overall aggression than girls. Bandura argued that the study proved that watching violent media can influence children's negative aggressive behavior.

Parental Concern

Studies such as Bandura's have fueled concerns about children's exposure to violence in film and television, including cartoons. By comparison, today's children are exposed to many more examples of aggressive behavior in the media. According to Eugene V. Beresin, director of Child and Adolescent Psychiatry Residency Training at Massachusetts General Hospital and McLean Hospital:

> Televised violence and the presence of television in American households have increased steadily over the years. In 1950, only 10% of American homes had a television. Today 99% of homes have televisions. In fact, more families have televisions than telephones. Over half of all children have a television set in their bedrooms. This gives a greater opportunity for children to view programs without parental supervision. Studies reveal that children watch approximately 28 hours of television a week, more time than they spend in school.[13]

"The typical American child will view more than 200,000 acts of violence, including more than 16,000 murders before age 18."[14]

— Eugene V. Beresin, director of Child and Adolescent Psychiatry Residency Training at Massachusetts General Hospital and McLean Hospital.

Indeed, today television appears to be far in the lead as the preferred media. According to a 2012 Nielsen study on media consumption, the average viewer watches 144 hours and 54 minutes, or the equivalent of more than six days, of television programming per month. By comparison, time spent on the Internet on a computer averages 28 hours, 29 minutes a month.

The increased access to media has again led to fears about its impact on children. Beresin comments that "the typical American child will view more than 200,000 acts of violence, including more than 16,000 murders before age 18. Television programs display 812 violent acts per hour; children's programming, particularly cartoons, displays up to 20 violent acts hourly."[14] Statistics from Common Sense Media, a media watchdog group, are similarly noteworthy. The group reports that by the time children finish elementary school, they will have seen eight thousand murders and one hundred thousand acts of violence on TV alone. The group also claims that teens who watch more than one hour of TV per day are four times more likely than other teens to commit aggressive acts in adulthood.

Although such statistics seem straightforward, they are open to interpretation and might be less dire than they first appear. David Trend, author of *The Myth of Media Violence*, suggests that there are degrees of violence, each with the potential to create a particular reaction—or no reaction at all. He explains:

Most people have no trouble calling to mind a violent image from a cop show, horror movie, or video game. But is media violence simply a matter of depicting physical harm? Does it need to be aggressive or intentional? What about accidents or natural disasters? Does psychological torment count? What about verbal or implied violence? Are there degrees of violence? Is justified violence better for viewers than the gratuitous variety? What about humorous violence? Sports? How about violent documentaries? Or the nightly news?[15]

Whatever the degree of media violence, most agree that violence is a staple in movies, television, and other forms of media. With the addition of cable, the American public's television choices have grown. Because it is available only by subscription, cable can show acts including nudity and graphic violence that are still not allowed on the regular airwaves. Shows such as the popular *Game of Thrones* or *True Blood* graphically depict killings on a grand scale, beheadings, and violent and disturbing sex scenes. According to *Los Angeles Times* movie critic Greg Braxton, "violence in television is, of course, not new. What is new—at least in this class of programming—is the unsparing detail with which it's being displayed, not to mention the inventiveness employed in showcasing the hacking, dismembering and killing."[16]

Desensitization

Another concern about the sheer number of exposures to violent media is that it desensitizes the viewer, who then tolerates more violence in the real world. Numerous studies have been configured to test this response. Psychologist Victor Cline studied children who previously had high and low exposure to television violence and showed each child a moderately violent film. Cline then measured the physiological responses of the children to the violent film. The children who previously had high exposure to television violence did not show heightened reaction to the film. The children with little or no exposure to television violence showed elevated physiological responses consistent with stress or fear. Cline concluded that previous exposure to media violence had desensitized the children.

Other studies have shown the same desensitization effect with adults. In 1984 a group of researchers showed slasher films to a sampling of college-aged men for five days. By the end of the week, the men rated the films as much less violent than they had at the start of the week. Such desensitization seemed to permanently change their attitudes toward real violence as well. When the men were shown a documentary about a sexual assault trial, they were far less sympathetic to the victim than a control group that had not watched the films.

Fear

Another focus of studies is whether media violence increases fear levels in both children and adults. In a 2002 study researcher Joanne Cantor found that children grew more fearful after watching film violence. For most children the fears diminished after a few days, while some continued to feel fear for months or longer. Other studies show that people who watch more television overestimate the amount of real violence in the world and

The average television viewer watches nearly 145 hours of programming per month. According to one recent study, not even Internet use comes close to this amount of time.

overestimate their chances of becoming a victim of violent crime.

In response to these and other studies, many professional organizations have lent their support to the view that media violence is harmful. In July 2000 the American Medical Association, the American Academy of Pediatrics, and other organizations made a joint statement to Congress: "Well over 1,000 studies point overwhelmingly to a causal connection between media violence and aggressive behavior in some children."[17] More recently, the International Society for Research on Aggression appointed a special commission to prepare a report on what is known about the effects of media violence based on scope of scientific evidence. The report, published in 2012, states:

> Over the past 50 years, a large number of studies conducted around the world have shown that watching violent television, watching violent films, or playing violent video games increases the likelihood for aggressive behavior. . . .

More than 15 meta-analyses have been published examining the links between media violence and aggression. . . . The results of all these meta-analyses show that exposure to media violence can increase not only aggressive behavior in a variety of forms, but also aggressive feelings, physiological arousal, and decreased prosocial behavior.[18]

The report notes that such effects have been seen in connection with all types of media, including TV, movies, video games, music, and cartoons.

While the preponderance of evidence seems to point to the dangers of a regular diet of media violence, studies are criticized for being inconclusive, flawed, or lacking a sizable enough link between media violence and real-world violence. As author and English professor Jonathan Gottschall says: "The evidence that violent media promotes violent behavior is actually pretty shaky. Violence is a great—perhaps the great—staple of the entertainment economy. As a society we guzzle down huge amounts of fake violence in television shows, novels, films, and video games. And yet, a determined fifty year search for real-world consequences of fictive violence hasn't found conclusive evidence of a causal linkage."[19]

> "Violence is a great—perhaps the great—staple of the entertainment economy. As a society we guzzle down huge amounts of fake violence in television shows, novels, films, and video games."[19]
>
> — Author and English professor Jonathan Gottschall.

Rash of Mass Shootings Brings Issue to the Fore

Despite the views of Gottschall and others who insist that violent entertainment does not cause real-world violence, many blame the rash of mass shootings on increasingly violent video games and television programming. Adam Lanza had dozens of weapons in his home, was a fan of the violent video game *Call of Duty*, and was said to be mentally disturbed and possibly showing symptoms of autism or Asperger's syndrome. All of these characteristics have been linked to the type of person who is most likely to be affected by media violence.

The Lanza case renewed talk of the dangers of media violence, but to some, such a link seems misguided. Speaking about the Sandy Hook school shooting, Iowa State professor Douglas Gentile bemoans the fact that media violence conversations happen only after these types of tragedies, which distorts the conversation: "Why is it the only time we talk about media violence is when there's a horrible event? Once we have a horrible tragedy like this, it really distorts the way we think about the issue . . . we have what I call a culprit mentality. 'What's the cause of this?' Well, it's never *the* cause. There's never one reason for anything like this. There's never one reason. Humans are complex."[20]

Some find such arguments unconvincing. Columnist Peggy Noonan writes: "Everyone who has warned for a quarter-century now that our national culture has become a culture of death—movies, TV shows, video-games drenched in blood and violence—has been correct. Deep down we all know it, as deep down we know our culture has a bad impact on the young and unstable who aren't sturdy enough to withstand and resist sick messages and imagery."[21]

Such opinions notwithstanding, more research may be needed to shed more definitive light on the subject. In January 2013 President Barack Obama ordered the Centers for Disease Control and Prevention (CDC) to conduct rigorous research into whether media violence in television, movies, and video games leads to gun violence and other forms of aggression. Obama stated: "We don't benefit from ignorance. We don't benefit from not knowing the science of this epidemic of violence. Congress should fund research into the effects violent video games have on young minds."[22] Obama pledged $10 million to the CDC for these efforts. But whether this effort yields anything more definitive remains to be seen.

"Everyone who has warned for a quarter-century now that our national culture has become a culture of death—movies, TV shows, videogames drenched in blood and violence—has been correct."[21]

— Columnist Peggy Noonan.

Facts

- In the early 1950s psychiatrist Frederic Wertham led a campaign to ban adventure comic and horror books, which he thought were corrupting based on his interviews with male juvenile delinquents—who were avid readers of these types of comics.

- A 1993 report by the National Research Council titled "Understanding and Preventing Violence" concluded that genetic and environmental factors were the primary causes of violent behavior.

- In 1992 Nassau County, New York, attempted—unsuccessfully—to pass an ordinance that banned the sale to minors of trading cards that depicted heinous crimes and criminals on the grounds that the cards caused psychological harm to minors.

- In the late 1980s and early 1990s, Memphis, Tennessee; Jacksonville, Florida; and other cities passed ordinances that banned minors from concerts that featured sexual or violent material.

- In a study in the 1960s, children who viewed humorous films were just as likely to exhibit aggressive tendencies as those children who viewed violent films. Children who viewed neutral films were less likely to behave aggressively.

Does Violent Media Cause Violent Behavior?

The courtroom during the trial of thirty-three-year-old Anders Breivik, who murdered sixty-nine young people in Norway in 2011, was filled with an eerie hush as he described training for the attacks by using the computer game *Call of Duty: Modern Warfare*. He recalled how he had developed "target acquisition" by playing the game:

> It consists of many hundreds of different tasks and some of these tasks can be compared with an attack, for real. That's why it's used by many armies throughout the world. It's very good for acquiring experience related to sights systems. . . . If you are familiar with a holographic sight, it's built up in such a way that you could have given it to your grandmother and she would have been a super marksman. It's designed to be used by anyone. In reality it requires very little training to use it in an optimal way. But of course it does help if you've practiced using a simulator.[23]

Breivik also said that he had taken time off from work in order to devote himself to playing another war game, *World of Warcraft*, for up to sixteen hours every day for a year. But he said it had nothing to do with preparing for the attack; he described it as a hobby: "Some people like to play golf, some like to sail, I played WoW. It had nothing to do with 22 July. It's not a world you are engulfed by. It's simply a hobby."[24]

Breivik's horrific story is not the only example of a shooter talking about these very same games. And yet millions of others play the games with no desire to go out and kill innocent people. This is at the heart of the debate over whether media violence causes real-world violence. The vast majority of people who play violent video games, watch violence on television, and view violent events on the Internet do not act out violently. This strongly suggests a more complicated relationship between media violence and real-world violence.

Difficulties in Establishing a Link

To date, dozens of studies of children and adults have found that people feel more violent and aggressive after viewing violence. Yet such research has failed to be predictive in the real world, in part because all the different types of research have flaws. Laboratory experiments may induce short-term effects in the lab but are criticized because their artificial circumstances are usually not transferable to the real world. Field studies have examined children's behavior after consuming violent entertainment, but almost all have yielded inconclusive and/or inconsistent results. Finally, correlational studies, usually conducted on a segment of the population or through a survey, may show a mathematical correlation but not proof that media violence causes real-life violence.

Additionally, scientists disagree over what constitutes violence and the degree of violence that might influence behavior. Attorney and author Marjorie Heins explains:

> Even those psychologists who believe that media violence is
> a significant influence on youthful attitudes and behavior
> do not agree about which violent images or ideas are harmful. Most acknowledge that contextual factors such as humor, plot, and theme (for example, whether the person us-

ing violence is punished) influence the ways that movies or TV shows are perceived. Others think that the stimulation created by a "hot" medium like television causes excitement or aggression regardless of the content of the program.[25]

Heins uses as an example the movie *Schindler's List*. While the movie graphically depicts the violent treatment of Jews by the Nazis during World War II, few would argue that it glorifies such violence. The audience instead feels moral outrage and sympathy for the Jews. The subjectivity of these distinctions illustrates how difficult it is to generalize about large-scale, long-term psychological or behavioral effects.

Violent Media and Gun Violence

Media scholars have long noted that many countries have equally or more violent media compared to the United States yet comparatively smaller amounts of gun violence. As web developer Ivan Boothe says:

> The UK—where *Grand Theft Auto* was developed—had just 58 murders from gun violence [in 2012], out of a population of 63 million. Australia, which has essentially the same film market as the United States—the top three movies in 2012 were *The Avengers*, *Dark Knight* and the latest James Bond movie—has had no mass shootings since 1996. . . . And in Japan, long seen as the source of the most violent video games in the world, the rate of gun violence deaths was 1,000 times smaller than in the United States (0.008 per 10,000 in Japan, vs. 10.3 per 100,000 in the U.S.).

Ivan Boothe, "5 Reasons Targeting 'Violence in the Media' Won't Help or Heal Our Society," Fellowship of Reconciliation, April 9, 2013. http://forusa.org.

There is also little scientific agreement on the exact nature of the effects of media violence. As Heins articulates:

> Some say the primary effect is imitation—the "modeling" behavior identified by the social learning school. Others think that media violence primarily desensitizes viewers—that is, makes them more callous about real-world violence. Still others subscribe to the "mean world" syndrome: they believe that violent entertainment or news reports cause people to become unduly fearful and to perceive the real world as being more brutal than it actually is. Finally, most studies in this area try to measure aggressive attitudes or behavior, not violence—and there is a big difference between the two.[26]

Heins and others note that it is difficult for researchers to distinguish acceptable aggression, a common human trait, from levels that go beyond the norm. Says Malte Elson, a research associate at the University of Münster in Germany:

> The problem is that measuring aggressiveness accurately is an intricate enterprise, and the variables observed in those studies often have very little resemblance with human experiences outside psychological laboratories. Measures of such behaviours typically include procedures like spicing a bowl of chili for someone else with the hotness of the sauce selected being the indicator of aggressiveness, or the volume of white noise that is used to punish another participant in a reaction time game. Other researchers measure other more distant facets of aggression, such as the accessibility of aggressive thoughts, e.g. how long it takes to identify words such as "gun" or "kill" after consuming violent media. Quite often the stimuli used in experiments as "violent" and "non-violent" media differ on so many levels that it is quite difficult to assess whether any obtained effects were caused by the violent content, and not something else.[27]

Generalizations about media violence and its effects can lead to flawed conclusions. Some violence, though graphic, stirs feelings of moral outrage and sympathy—as in the 1993 movie Schindler's List *(pictured), which graphically depicted the violent treatment of Jews by the Nazis during World War II.*

Many Types of Aggression

As these researchers state, not everyone agrees on what constitutes aggression. Some forms of aggression, such as verbal assaults, are considered acceptable in situations involving self-defense or standing up for oneself. The same can be said for some instances of violence. Most people accept violence if it is taken as an act of self-defense. Violence is also seen as acceptable when it occurs in sports such as hockey, football, and boxing. In addition, because research studies cannot have real violence occur, psychologists must use film violence and then extrapolate from their studies to determine what acts constitute aggression. Or sometimes they rely on reports of others, such as teachers or parents.

In studies of violence and aggression, pinpointing cause and effect is also extremely difficult for researchers. Just on the seemingly simple question of violent media, scientists must speculate on whether people who consume violent media become more violent or whether people who are violent tend to consume more violent media.

Heins and other researchers have found that in some studies causality is simply implied and cannot be definitively proved. "Finding a 'statistically significant' correlation between two 'variables'—aggressive behavior and preference for violent television, for example—simply means that the two are found together too often to occur purely by chance. But the correlation may not be very large; it may not exist in most, or even a substantial number, of cases."[28]

In addition, no study has yet to examine acts like Breivik's in Norway as acts of a mentally disturbed mind rather than simply a reaction to violent games. Researchers suspect that a certain subset of the population may be more prone to extreme violent acts, and members of this segment may be more vulnerable to acting out the violence they see.

Flaws Do Not Invalidate Studies

Despite the flaws of past media studies, some researchers believe that the sheer preponderance of evidence cannot be ignored. Taken together, these studies indicate a link between media violence and real-world violence. According to testimony presented before the Senate Judiciary Committee by David S. Bickham of the Center on Media and Child Health at Children's Hospital Boston and Harvard Medical School: "Taken alone, no study is perfect. Even the best study design can be criticized for the limitations of its method. Taken together, however, each study about media violence provides a piece of a single puzzle that all interlock to reveal one picture. In this case, the picture is clear—using violent media contributes to children's violent behavior. A variety of complementary methodologies that have resulted in similar findings have been used to generate this overall conclusion."[29]

A classic study, called the "Rip Van Winkle" study, is still considered one of the most definitive in proving the media violence/real-life violence link. Beginning in 1960 researcher Leonard D. Eron followed eight hundred children from the age of eight through adulthood. Eron interviewed the subjects every ten years.

Mentally Ill May Be More Vulnerable to Media Violence

Tom Grimes is a professor of mass communication and an adjunct research professor at Texas State University. Grimes has studied media violence extensively; he describes his research findings that suggest that the mentally ill may be much more prone to negative reactions after viewing violent media:

> None of the nearly 2,000 media violence studies over the past 80 years has tried to diagnostically separate people who might be mentally unwell from those without a diagnosable ailment.
>
> In a series of studies my colleagues and I conducted over 15 years, we performed medical diagnoses on children ages 12–18, separating those suffering a common cluster of ailments—disruptive behavior disorders [DBDs]—from kids with no diagnosis. DBDs refer to behaviors that include explosive, violent temper tantrums, which can be provoked by watching media violence. In fact, in one of our studies, one DBD-afflicted child tried to stab an orderly with a ballpoint pen after seeing a scene from Clint Eastwood's *In the Line of Fire*. In the other group, children were bored by what they saw, were entertained, or were made anxious, but they were not psychologically harmed by it.

Tom Grimes, "Define Violence in the Media; Column," *USA Today*, January 20, 2013. www.usatoday.com.

Though Eron died in 2007, the study is ongoing; the subjects were last interviewed in 2000. Eron and colleagues reported that "youngsters at age 8 who were not aggressive at school but were watching violent TV at home were by age 18 significantly more aggressive than youngsters who at age 8 were aggressive at school but not watching violent TV at home. . . . The kids who watched violent TV at age 8 are significantly more aggressive by the time they reach age 30—more criminal convictions, more abuse of spouses, more drunk-driving convictions."[30] Eron's study was one of the few that followed its subjects for so long and yielded such clear results.

Studies similar to the Rip Van Winkle study have been repeated in other parts of the world. A 2013 study from New Zealand published in *Pediatrics* found that excessive television viewing in childhood and the early teen years is correlated to increased risk of criminal convictions and antisocial behaviors in young adults.

Desensitized to Violence

A 2010 study used magnetic resonance imaging (MRI) technology to view the brain while adolescents watched videos that contained varying degrees of aggressive behavior. Lead researchers discovered that repeated exposure to the videos decreased brain response, indicating that the test subjects became desensitized to the violence over time. Researcher Maren Strenziok and her colleagues found that "aggressive media activates an emotion-attention network that has the capability to blunt emotional responses . . . which may restrict the linking of the consequences of aggression with an emotional response, and therefore potentially promotes aggressive attitudes and behavior."[31]

It is this desensitization that has many people concerned. Violence without a moral context, or some video games and movies seen as entertainment, could hardwire young peoples' brains to react to real-life situations in a more violent way. In its 2012 report the Media Violence Commission concluded that such hardwiring could "result in changes to attitudes and beliefs about aggression, such as seeing aggression as a more acceptable response to provocations. Changes to thoughts and feelings can result in changes in behavior, but not necessarily in a mechanistic way—more by changing the odds that a provocation will be met with an aggressive response."[32]

Justifiable Violence

Even in media where the hero is the only one to use violence and uses it justly, as in avenging a wrong, the violence may still prove to have a poor influence on young people, according to some researchers. Movies and other media that reinforce a good guy/bad guy worldview may still not be healthy for children, whose moral universe is still developing. Says Michelle Garrison, an investigator at Seattle Children's Research Institute Center for Child Health, Behavior, and Development: "If a child sees himself as the 'good guy,' then anyone who disagrees with him must be a 'bad guy'—and this black-and-white thinking doesn't leave much room for trying to see it from the other side, or working out a win-win compromise. . . . On the other hand, if a child starts seeing himself as a 'bad guy,' then it may no longer feel like it's about choices and actions that can change."[33]

This predetermined moral world can still lead to unacceptable violence. Garrison states: "With both preschool and school-aged children, studies have found that they are more likely to imitate the violence they see on screen if someone they see as a 'good guy' is using the violence to solve a problem, especially if there are no realistic consequences for the violence."[34]

Even those who believe that media violence influences future real-life violence know that it is not the sole factor. Nevertheless, Bickham believes it is a significant factor. "Sound scientific research in this field does not claim that media violence is the sole cause of human aggression. Nor does it claim that media violence is necessarily the original or most important cause—we all know that human aggression has been around much longer than violent video games. Violent media is, however, a substantial, pervasive, and controllable contributor to children's aggression and violent behaviors."[35]

And yet a number of compelling studies seem to indicate that the role of media violence is less significant than researchers like

"If a child sees himself as the 'good guy,' then anyone who disagrees with him must be a 'bad guy'—and this black-and-white thinking doesn't leave much room for trying to see it from the other side, or working out a win-win compromise."[33]

— Michelle Garrison, an investigator at Seattle Children's Research Institute Center for Child Health, Behavior, and Development.

Bickham make it out to be. A 2013 study from Texas A&M International University found that genetics and environment are far greater predictors of future violent behavior than watching violent media. As lead researcher Christopher J. Ferguson, university chair and associate professor of psychology, says: "We basically find that genetics and some social issues combine to predict later adult arrests. . . . Despite ongoing concerns about media influences, media exposure does not seem to function as a risk factor for adult criminality."[36]

Ferguson and others, then, believe the mix of characteristics that lead to violence is much more complex and cannot simply be attributed to media. Ferguson contends, "People may object morally to some of the content that exists in the media, but the question is whether the media can predict criminal behavior. The answer seems to be no." The study found that factors such as a child's environment, family, peers, and socioeconomic status could better predict future criminality: "Genetics alone don't seem to trigger criminal behavior, but in combination with harsh upbringing, you can see negative outcomes. . . . In our sample, experiencing maternal warmth seemed to reduce the impact of genetics on adult criminality."[37]

A compelling argument for media violence being less impactful is that many studies prove it is primarily a phenomenon isolated to the United States. As Paul Waldman writes in the *American Prospect*:

> If exposure to violent media was a significant determinant of real-world violence, then since media culture is now global, every country would have about the same level of violence, and of course they don't. Japan would be the most violent society on earth. Have you seen the crazy stuff the Japanese watch and play? . . . But in fact, Japan is at or near the bottom among industrialized countries in every category of violent crime, from murder to rape to robbery. There are many reasons, some of them cultural, some of them practical . . . but the point is that even if all that violent media is having an effect on Japanese psyches,

"Violent media is . . . a substantial, pervasive, and controllable contributor to children's aggression and violent behaviors."[35]

— David S. Bickham, staff scientist at the Center on Media and Child Health at Children's Hospital Boston.

the effect is so small that it doesn't make much of a difference on a societal level.[38]

Benefits to Violent Media?

Some researchers even argue that media violence can be beneficial. Viewing violence, even participating in it in the form of video games, may produce a release of emotions similar to the theory of catharsis, attributed to the ancient Greek philosopher Aristotle. Aristotle believed that when people saw tragic or violent scenes portrayed in plays, they experienced an emotional release that purged them of similar angry or hateful feelings. As Jonathan Gottschall says:

> Virtually without exception, when the villain of a story kills, his violence is condemned. When the hero kills, he does so righteously. Fiction preaches that violence is only acceptable under defined circumstances—to protect the good and the weak from the bad and the strong. Some games, like *Grand Theft Auto,* seem to glorify and reward bad behavior (although in a semi-satirical spirit), but those games are the notorious exceptions that prove the general rule. What Steven King says of horror stories in his book *Danse Macabre,* broadly applies to all forms of imaginary violence: "The horror story, beneath its fangs and fright wig, is really as conservative as an Illinois Republican in a three-piece pinstriped suit. . . . It's main purpose is to reaffirm the virtues of the norm by showing us what awful things happen to people who venture into taboo lands. Within the framework of most horror tales we find a moral code so strong it would make a Puritan smile."[39]

Aristotle also believed that viewing violent and tragic acts was necessary for human sanity—humans needed to feel a sense of heightened emotion and vicariously live through the characters in order to renew their sense of justice and faith in mankind. Aristotle's beliefs have been echoed in arguments of media violence today. Ac-

"People may object morally to some of the content that exists in the media, but the question is whether the media can predict criminal behavior. The answer seems to be no."[37]

— Christopher J. Ferguson, associate professor at Texas A&M International University.

Two young boys play Grand Theft Auto, a game that glorifies bad behavior. Many other video games actually reflect traditional themes of good and bad through characters who try to protect the good and the weak against the bad and the strong.

cording to the Free Expression Policy Project: "Violence has been a subject in literature and the arts since the beginning of human civilization. In part, this simply reflects the unfortunate realities of the world. But it's also likely that our fascination with violence satisfies some basic human needs. The adrenalin rush, the satisfactions of imagination, fantasy, and vicarious adventure, probably explain why millions of nonviolent people enjoy violent entertainment."[40]

Call for Research

The debate over media violence and real violence continues. In 2013, in fact, the CDC was tasked with funding future research on the topic. The CDC, the Institute of Medicine, and the National Research Council will focus on research that works with three- to five-year-olds in an attempt to discover a definitive link, or lack thereof, between media violence and future gun violence. In justifying the new research, the CDC explains:

> While the vast majority of research on the effects of violence in media has focused on violence portrayed in television and movies, more recent research has expanded to include music, video games, social media, and the Internet—outlets that consume more and more of young people's days. However, in more than 50 years of research, no study has focused on firearm violence as a specific outcome of violence in media. As a result, a direct relationship between violence in media and real-life firearm violence has not been established and will require additional research.[41]

Whether the CDC study will provide new answers to this question remains to be seen.

Facts

- According to the website Parenting.com, children are more likely to imitate media violence committed by heroes as opposed to villains.

- A study of violent movies between 1995 and 2005 found that violent crime decreased on days with the largest theater audiences viewing violent movies.

- Joanne Cantor, a professor at the University of Wisconsin at Madison who studies media violence, asserts that her research has found that violent media makes children more fearful of the world and causes an increase in sleep disturbances.

- One study of children by J. Cantor and B.J. Wilson found that repeated exposure to characters in, for example, the *Incredible Hulk* or the *Wizard of Oz* can make children less fearful.

- A study published in the journal *Pediatrics* in the late 1980s found more aggressive behavior in children after viewing nonviolent shows like *Sesame Street* and *Mr. Rogers' Neighborhood*.

- According to the Free Expression Policy Project, every federal appellate court that has addressed the issue of violent entertainment has rejected the premise that research proves a causal relationship between violent media and violent behavior.

Are Violent Video Games Harming Youth?

Many observers, social scientists, and media critics blame recent school shootings on violent video games. One of the most recent incidents was Adam Lanza's murderous rampage in Connecticut. Lanza was an avid gun collector and a fan of violent video games such as *Call of Duty* and *World of Warcraft*.

While such examples seem damning, others contend that they prove little. Game designer Tadhg Kelly argues that all games feature some sort of violence, but it is functional rather than real violence. The functional violence of a game might involve stealing, killing, or using some other means to destroy one's opponent. In chess, for instance, players use their men to wipe out the opponent's resources to capture the king. In *Risk*, players attempt to use armies to gain world domination. Video games are no different; players use violence to compete and win the game. Kelly contends that when he designs a game, he attempts to engage all parts of the brain in the reality of the play—but it never stops being a game. "The first time you defeat a minotaur in *God of War* through the special move of pressing X repeatedly

"The first time you defeat a minotaur in God of War through the special move of pressing X repeatedly to drive a sword into its throat, it's pretty bloody and spectacular. The tenth time you do it, it just signifies a win. As you see the same violent effects again and again, their power quickly diminishes."[42]

— Game developer Tadhg Kelly.

to drive a sword into its throat, it's pretty bloody and spectacular. The tenth time you do it, it just signifies a win. As you see the same violent effects again and again, their power quickly diminishes."[42]

Watching Versus Playing

Yet many do not agree with Kelly that violent video games never result in violent action. A chief argument made by those who support the view that violent video games have played a role in increasing aggression and in motivating school shootings is that violent video games are distinctly different than other forms of media violence. A video gamer actively participates in violence—shooting, killing, and maiming, rather than passively watching it as one would in a movie or television program.

While few studies have examined this theory, one was completed in 2012 by Ohio State University professor Brad Bushman. Bushman divided French university students into groups of thirty-five: One group played a violent game, one group played a nonviolent game, and one group watched the violent game. Later, when tested, the young men who had played the violent video game were significantly more aggressive than those who just watched. As Bushman says, "It's a beautiful study because they saw exactly the same violent images . . . which would not be the case if one watched a movie and another played a video game. They saw exactly the same violent images, but the players were more aggressive than the watchers. So we need more studies like that."[43]

Body of Research Confirms Link to Aggression

One effort to expand on research into the effects of violent video games was undertaken in 2010 by Craig Anderson, a professor of psychology at Iowa State University. Anderson's analysis of other study findings (called meta-analysis) confirms that violent video games stimulate aggression in players. According to Anderson and his colleague Douglas Gentile, associate professor of child psychology also at Iowa State University: "The most comprehensive meta-analysis of violent video games—including more than 130 studies of more than 130,000 people—found consistent evidence that violent games increase desensitization, aggressive thoughts, feel-

Violent Video Games Can Benefit Kids

According to Common Sense Media, a website that parents can use to vet children's media consumption, fully 68 percent of video games show depictions of violence. Most children, moreover, start playing video games around age four, and many graduate to violent video games such as *Grand Theft Auto* or *Call of Duty* by the early teen years. Many video game researchers, such as Cheryl K. Olson, believe that there are positive effects of this ubiquitous pastime. These include allowing the user to play the role of hero, to learn to delay gratification, to be persistent, to solve problems, to learn to cope with frustration, and to blow off steam. Author and English professor Jonathan Gottschall also agrees that the dire predictions about video game violence are overblown. Gottschall states that "adventure style video games almost always insert players into imaginative scenarios where they play the role of hero bravely confronting the forces of chaos and destruction. When you play a video game you aren't training to be a spree shooter; you are training to be the good guy who races to place himself between evil and its victims."

Jonathan Gottschall, "What *Should* We Be Worried About?," *Edge*, 2013. www.edge.org.

ings, physiology, and behaviors, and decrease helpful behaviors. Even the few scientists who claim there is nothing to worry about find very similar results in their small-scale meta-analyses."[44]

L. Rowell Huesmann, a professor of psychology at the University of Michigan, comments on Anderson's research and how mass media, including video games, have become important socializers of young people:

Mass media exposures contribute to a child's socialization, just as exposures to family, peers, and community contribute. . . . It requires a tortuous logic to believe that children and adolescents are affected by what they observe in their living room, through the front window of their house, in their classroom, in their neighborhood, and among their peers, but are not affected by what they observe in movies, on television, or in the video games they play. Yet many have argued just such a view in opposition to researchers who conclude that media violence stimulates aggression. Furthermore, the most vociferous opposition has been expressed against conclusions that violent video games might be teaching youths to behave more aggressively. The meta-analysis by Anderson et al. is the best yet in proving beyond a reasonable doubt that exposure to video game violence increases the risk that the observer will behave more aggressively and violently in the future.[45]

Huesmann also linked violent video games to aggressive fantasies. In a three-year study Huesmann and colleagues surveyed students in second, fourth, and ninth grade three times at one-year intervals, measuring how much time they spent playing violent video games. Researchers also measured the students' aggressive tendencies with questions like "When you get mad, sometimes do you daydream about the things you would like to do to the person you're mad at, like hitting, damaging their things, or getting them into trouble?" Researchers found that "habitual playing of violent video games by children and adolescents is related to engaging in more aggressive behavior, and to more aggression-related cognitions such as . . . fantasies about aggression."[46]

Another study examined the link between violent games and future crime. A 2012 Iowa State University study of 227 violent juvenile offenders in Pennsylvania concluded that a connection existed between playing violent video games and delinquent behavior. The average offender studied had committed at least nine serious acts of violence against another person during the

"It requires a tortuous logic to believe that children and adolescents are affected by what they observe in their living room, through the front window of their house, in their classroom, in their neighborhood, and among their peers, but are not affected by what they observe in movies, on television, or in the video games they play."[45]

— L. Rowell Huesmann, a professor of psychology and communications studies at the University of Michigan.

One study identified a link between delinquent behavior by juvenile offenders (such as the young offenders pictured here) and violent video game play. Although video games might not actually cause violent behavior the study found they can increase the likelihood of it occurring.

previous year. The researchers concluded that while violent video games could not be determined to have a causal effect on violent behavior, they proved to be a significant risk factor. In particular, the researchers were careful to control for factors such as upbringing. Professor of sociology Matt DeLisi argues, "When critics say, 'Well it's probably not video games, it's probably how antisocial they are,' we can address that directly because we controlled for a lot of things that we know matter. . . . Even if you account for the child's sex, age, race, the age they were first referred to juvenile court—which is a very powerful effect—and a bunch of other media effects, like screen time and exposure. Even with all of that, the video game measure still mattered."[47]

DeLisi, though cautioning parents that not all kids who play violent video games will become violent, remarked that, "I think parents need to be truthful and honest about who their children are in terms of their psychiatric functioning. . . . If you have a kid who is antisocial, who is a little bit vulnerable to influence, giving him something that allows them to escape into themselves for a long period of time isn't a healthy thing."[48]

Video Games' Influence Is Profound

Some research has focused on how young people who play hours of violent video games can enter into a self-centered, isolated fantasy world that encourages real aggression. This fantasy world can also promote violence as being justified and rewarded. Such a view of violence may encourage school shootings. In a game environment, players participate in massive shooting sprees where victims are viewed as deserving to be killed for their transgressions. Some researchers believe that it is just common sense to understand that, especially for a young person who may suffer from mental instability, the leap to using real violence against people who have transgressed against him or her may seem logical. The Canadian website Media Smarts concludes, "Given the focus of these games on weaponry, the paranoia-inducing corridors that are typical of game environments, and the role of the player as lone judge, jury, and executioner, it isn't difficult to see the line of thinking that links these types of games to the idea of mass violence."[49]

Indeed, such factors seem to come together in many real-life shootings. In the Virginia Polytechnic Institute massacre of 2007, Seung-Hui Cho shot and killed thirty-two people and wounded seventeen others in two separate attacks, approximately two hours apart, before committing suicide. Cho, a college senior from Blacksburg, Virginia, had been diagnosed with a severe anxiety disorder, of which the university remained unaware because of privacy laws. Many people in Cho's life, including his mother, a school counselor, and several of his professors, had said that Cho needed psychiatric treatment. In Cho's case, no evidence of violent video game play turned up. However, this did not stop the media commentators from immediately speculating

"Given the focus of these games on weaponry, the paranoia-inducing corridors that are typical of game environments, and the role of the player as lone judge, jury, and executioner, it isn't difficult to see the line of thinking that links these types of games to the idea of mass violence."[49]

— Media Smarts, a Canadian website.

on the relationship between violent video games and real-life violence, particularly in someone who has a disturbed state of mind. Phil McGraw, the Dr. Phil of TV fame, commenting on the Virginia Tech shootings on *Larry King Live*, April 16, 2007, argued:

> Common sense tells you that if these kids are playing video games, where they're on a mass killing spree in a video game, it's glamorized on the big screen, it's become part of the fiber of our society. You take that and mix it with a psychopath, a sociopath or someone suffering from mental illness and add in a dose of rage, the suggestibility is too high.
>
> And we're going to have to start dealing with that. We're going to have to start addressing those issues and recognizing that the mass murderers of tomorrow are the children of today that are being programmed with this massive violence overdose.[50]

Those who suffer from mental illness are not the only ones who are vulnerable to the influence of violent media, some commentators believe. The entire media landscape is violent, they argue, and this violence permeates society, making aggression and violence far more acceptable. Such commentators then, see video game violence as reinforcing the idea that one must respond to violence with violence. When a child's world is filled with violent television and video games, and even reinforced by bullies at school, it is difficult for him or her to grow up believing and trusting in the goodness and kindness of others. In playing video games that revel in killing, maiming, and torturing others, Jenny McCartney, columnist for the *Telegraph*, makes the point that: "The instinctive objection remains, and it is indeed rooted in morality: the sense that it is wrong for anyone, child or adult, to spend long hours electronically rehearsing the prolonged agony and detailed humiliation of other human beings for their own amusement. It is insidiously corrupting to their view of themselves and other people."[51]

"The instinctive objection remains, and it is indeed rooted in morality: the sense that it is wrong for anyone, child or adult, to spend long hours electronically rehearsing the prolonged agony and detailed humiliation of other human beings for their own amusement."[51]

— Jenny McCartney, a columnist for the *Telegraph*.

Dearth of Reliable Research

Not all agree, however, that the research clearly points to violent video games as a factor in increased aggression and school shootings. Many scientists and media scholars have concluded that while it may be true that video games heighten aggression, this in no way proves that such aggression leads to violence. As media scholar Jason Schreier writes on the gaming website Kotaku, "While there are no documented scientific links between video games and criminal violence, the question of whether violent video games lead to aggression has been hotly debated. (That distinction between criminal violence and aggression is critical. Science has yet to show any links between video games and violence, but violent games may have a more subtle effect on children: for example, they could make a child more inclined to bully or spread rumors about his peers)."[52]

Christopher J. Ferguson says the recent meta-analyses and other studies that link video games and aggressiveness suffer from flaws that destroy their credibility. One flaw, Ferguson argues, is that the studies are mostly composed of university students. He believes these students taint the research because they are more likely to figure out what the study seeks to learn and act accordingly. "These college students are guessing what they're supposed to do and doing it, in order to get their extra credit."[54]

Other flaws involve scientific validity and interpretation of data. Ferguson believes that methods for testing aggression lack scientific validity; they are inconsistent and poor predictors of violence in the real world. Additionally, most studies leave too much up to the researchers' interpretation of the data and so cannot be relied upon. Ferguson cites the noise test given to the French students in the Bushman study as an example. After playing violent video games, the students were asked to subject other students who lost at games to a prolonged, unpleasant noise. Ferguson claims that it is difficult to extrapolate aggression based on such vague reactions. "From the same noise burst test, you can

"It has been increasingly recognized that much of the early research on VVG [violent video games] linking them to aggression was problematic."[55]

— Christopher J. Ferguson, associate professor of psychology at Texas A&M International University.

Virginia State Police make their way to the site of a 2007 mass shooting at Virginia Polytechnic Institute. Although investigators found no evidence that the shooter played violent video games, media commentators used the massacre as yet another reason to discuss the effects of violent video games.

either show that video games increase aggression, decrease aggression, or have no effect at all. . . . So the concern is that researchers that have a particular belief system are just picking outcomes."[54]

These flaws make current research invalid, Ferguson concludes. "It has been increasingly recognized that much of the early research on VVG [violent video games] linking them to aggression was problematic: most studies used outcome measures that had nothing to do with real-life aggression and failed to control carefully for other important variables, such as family violence, mental health issues or even gender in many studies."[55]

Ferguson's own 2013 study followed 165 ten- to fourteen-year-olds over a three-year-period and found no long-term link between playing violent video games and dating violence. Ferguson contends that simple statistical data proves that the video game effect is false. "Though video game sales have skyrocketed, youth violence plummeted to its lowest levels in 40 years,"[56] he contends. In addition, young people are adept at distinguishing between fantasy and the real world. For instance, no child reaches adulthood still believing in Santa Claus and the Easter Bunny.

Kelly echoes this view: "As players we may get immersed in a game world, even wrapped up in its fiction, but we never lose our sense of self. Play is a mock activity, an illusion, and we are able to distinguish between reality and fantasy."[57] Statistics seem to bear out Kelly's conclusions. *Call of Duty*, the violent video game that Lanza was so fond of, sold 15 million copies in the United States—half of all gamers own a copy. Yet none of these millions has appeared in the news as a mass killer.

Correlation Versus Causality

While studies have demonstrated a link between aggression and video games, this link does not prove causality—that violent video games will lead to violent behavior. In fact, other factors are likely more important in predicting future violence. A 2004 study at Massachusetts General Hospital, led by video game violence expert Cheryl K. Olson, studied the reasons students play violent video games. She found that middle schoolers who played violent video games sought them out to relieve, rather than spur, their anger. In addition, violent video games were seen as more fun than other games, although not specifically because of the violence. Reasons cited included: better variety of character and weaponry options; higher skill level to play; possibility of playing with multiple players; increasing competition; and social interaction.

Olson's interviews found that many kids played video games for emotional release. Sixty-two percent of boys and 44 percent of girls said that they played the games to relax, to ease anger or stress, and to forget problems or ease loneliness. One student said, "Getting wrapped up in a violent game, it's good. 'Cause if you mad, when you come home, you can take your anger out on the people in the game."[58] In addition to relieving bad feelings, many students said that it was simply fun: "It's something to do when I'm bored,"[59] was a frequent answer.

As Olson and others contend, violent games may act as a release for aggressive feelings that could otherwise erupt in the real world. Many biologists believe that such aggressive feelings in ado-

The Most Violent Video Games

Common Sense Media describes the popular video game *Call of Duty: Black Ops II*, which the group identifies as one of the ten most violent video games on the market today:

> This gritty, extremely violent military first-person shooter involves constant killing using realistic weapons, with blood and gore pouring across the screen during more intense scenes. Cinematic sequences can be even more dramatic and graphic, with soldiers and civilians alike dying in horrible ways, including graphic melee kills, people burning to death, civilians killed in crossfire, torture and a shipping container filled with rotting corpses. In one scene, the player steps into the shoes of a villain and goes on a murderous rampage against soldiers, the screen turning red with blood rage as he takes damage. This M-rated game also has frequent profanity, some sexual themes and drug use.

Common Sense Media, "10 Most Violent Video Games (and 10 Plus Alternatives)," *Huffington Post*, June 24, 2013. www.huffingtonpost.com.

lescence are normal, biologically driven behaviors. Olson writes, "Historically, boys and men have been particularly drawn to group experiences of vicarious violence, from war games to horror films to boxing or wrestling matches. . . . Boys in particular often use rough-and-tumble play fighting to establish dominance and a social pecking order, with no intention to harm. Video game play could serve as another arena for the developmentally appropriate battle for status among peers."[60]

This link between boys' normal aggression and video games can become exaggerated by the media, making the link appear more causal than it is. As Ferguson says:

We focus, irrationally, on it [playing violent video games] in cases where the perpetrator is a young male [shooter] like Adam Lanza, since almost all young males consume violent media. But when the perpetrator is an older male, such as 62-year-old William Spengler, who killed two volunteer firefighters the week after Sandy Hook, or the rare woman, such as Amy Bishop, the 44-year-old biology professor who killed three at her university in 2010, video games simply aren't mentioned. This kind of confirmation bias allows us to think video games are a common thread when they are not.[61]

More Research Needed

Even the Supreme Court could not agree that video game violence produced violent behavior. In 2011 it struck down a California law that barred the sale or rental of violent video games to people under the age of eighteen. The court rejected the law on First Amendment grounds, yet acknowledged that further review could reveal new information. Justice Samuel A. Alito Jr. writes, "We should take into account the possibility that developing technology may have important societal implications that will become apparent with time."[62]

Most agree with Alito that more research is needed on how these games affect youth. More important, perhaps, is research untainted by strong bias one way or another. According to *Time* magazine writer Matt Peckham, "While the research is clear that violent video games don't incite people to pick up guns, strap on bulletproof vests and go on mass killing sprees, it's wrong to assume we shouldn't be asking and studying how changing media/mediums might affect us. So I cringe a little when I read stories where one side melodramatically absolves itself of any responsibility, while another pens acid rebuttals that amount to one-tenths evidence and nine-tenths snark."[63]

Facts

- According to a 2013 study published in the journal *Psychosomatic Medicine: Journal of Biobehavioral Medicine*, teenage boys who play violent video games are not only more prone to aggressive behavior but also suffer higher anxiety levels and sleep disturbances.

- In 2000 St. Louis County passed a law to restrict minors' use of violent video games in arcades. The law was ultimately overturned on the grounds that video games fall in the category of constitutionally protected speech.

- A study presented in August 2013 at a Society for Personality and Social Psychology symposium reported that violent video games may increase impulsive behavior in users.

- A large study published in 2009 in the journal *Psychological Science* found that 8.5 percent of video gamers exhibited pathological patterns of usage, including spending more than twenty-four hours a week playing video games and having trouble paying attention in school.

- In August 2005 the American Psychological Association passed the "Resolution on Violence in Video Games and Interactive Media" that cautioned video gamers and parents that violent video games may be more damaging than violent television and called for a reduction of violence in video games.

What Is the Impact of Sexual Violence in the Media?

Movies and television have long used the plot device of the damsel in distress. This device dates as far back as the 1914 movie serial *Perils of Pauline*, in which Pauline was often found to be facing death at the end of every film so that audiences would come back the next week to find out what happened. The *Perils of Pauline* is tame compared to the frightening female-themed story lines found in modern media; they are more graphic and violent than ever, involving murder and sexual violence. And while ratings systems are supposed to limit teens' and children's exposure to such violence, they are not sheltered from it. Contemporary viewers—including children and teens—are exposed to thousands of murders, rapes, and sexual assaults each year in the media, including news sources on the Internet and television. According to a 2009 report by the Parents Television Council (PTC), in television alone, there has been a "significant increase in the incidence of female victimization; an increase in the depiction of teen girls as victims; an increase in the use of female victimization as a punch line in comedy series; and an increase in the depiction of intimate partner violence."[64]

The PTC report also found that violence against women on television is increasing at rates far greater than for violence in general. In fact, the report found that most major television networks showed a dramatic increase in the number of story lines between 2004 and 2009 that hinged on violence against women. During this same period, there was a 400 percent increase in depiction of teen girls as victims. The report concluded, "By depicting violence against women with increasing frequency, or as a trivial, even humorous matter, the networks may be contributing to an atmosphere in which young people view aggression and violence against women as normative, even acceptable."[65] Many observers believe that sex linked with violence may have a particularly pernicious impact on viewers, especially children.

According to a 2013 report authored by Marcus Berzofsky and others for the Bureau of Justice Statistics, roughly two women per thousand were raped or sexually assaulted in the years between 2005 and 2010. In that same period, women aged thirty-four and younger who lived in lower-income households and who lived in rural areas experienced some of the highest rates of sexual violence. Seventy-eight percent of those victimized were assaulted by a family member, intimate partner, friend, or acquaintance. Whether these statistics are linked to the increase in media violence, however, is difficult to prove.

Some believe that such a link is real and that it is fueled by portrayals of women in film and on television. In her role as goodwill ambassador for the United Nations Development Fund for Women, actress Nicole Kidman testified before a 2009 congressional subcommittee considering legislation to mitigate violence against women. Kidman stated her view that Hollywood has contributed to this violence by portraying women as weak sex objects.

Early Studies

Much work on the link between real violence against women and television and movie violence was conducted in the 1980s by re-

"By depicting violence against women with increasing frequency, or as a trivial, even humorous matter, the [television] networks may be contributing to an atmosphere in which young people view aggression and violence against women as normative, even acceptable."[65]

— Parents Television Council.

searcher Neil M. Malamuth, a social psychologist at the University of California at Los Angeles. Malamuth noted that some sexual scenes are portrayed as though the woman finds the sexual assault alluring, resisting at first but then giving in: "When sexual violence is portrayed, there is frequently the suggestion that, despite initial resistance, the victim secretly desired the abusive treatment and eventually derived pleasure from it. This provides a built-in justification for aggression that would otherwise be considered unjustifiable."[66]

Malamuth and others believe that the sheer amount of sexual violence in the media can influence changes in attitudes in men. Young men may believe that women enjoy being pursued and forced to accept their physical attentions even when they explicitly tell their pursuer they are not interested. When these attitudes are silently condoned by society and are accepted by peers and family, a man who is prone to violence can interpret this acceptance as granting a license to violence. According to Malamuth, "Such atti-

Actress Nicole Kidman speaks to the media. In her role as goodwill ambassador for the United Nations Development Fund for Women, Kidman has testified that Hollywood portrayals of women as sex objects contribute to real-life sexual violence against women.

tudes might contribute to stranger and date rape, a desire, not acted upon, to be sexually aggressive, sanctioning the sexual aggression of others, or sexist and discriminatory acts. Even when not translated into violent behavior, such effects have wide social implications."[67]

Thus, the effect of media violence reinforces negative ideas about female sexuality. Mass media images and depictions influence a man's attitudes and perceptions, for example, and if that particular man has experienced other environmental factors, such as an abusive childhood, he may act out his aggression. Another example may be that of a man who may not personally act out his violent desires but will look away or condone sexual violence against women by other men. Such attitudes could surface if the man is on a jury during a rape trial or in conversations with other men who advocate hurting women. Malamuth believes that a number of factors contribute to a man wanting to hurt or rape a woman, and mass media may be one of those factors. He and others believe that of the many factors involved in violence against women, curbing media violence is one of the easiest to remedy.

Other early groundbreaking research seems to corroborate Malamuth's views. Researcher Edward Donnerstein performed a study with college-aged men in the 1980s. The subjects viewed R-rated violent slasher films, X-rated nonviolent pornographic films, or R-rated nonviolent teenage sex films. Men who had viewed the violent films were less sympathetic to the film victim and to rape victims in general. Donnerstein concluded, "If you take normal males and expose them to graphic violence against women in R-rated films, the research doesn't show that they'll commit acts of violence against women. It doesn't say they will go out and commit rape. But it does demonstrate that they become less sensitized to violence against women, they have less sympathy for rape victims, and their perceptions and attitudes and values about violence change."[68]

Slasher Films

These early studies spawned new research into today's films and television depictions of sexual violence. One genre studied by researcher Andrew Welsh at the University of Albany was the slasher film. These films depict an evil main character who slashes his

"Women Are Prey"

A campaign to censor the content of music videos and lyrics was begun by the National Sexual Violence Research Center in 2012. The center believes that sexually explicit music videos and lyrics are one of the most pernicious factors in encouraging cultural attitudes that lead to the victimization of women. Writing about the campaign, journalist Kayley Gillespie comments:

> Human sexuality has emotional, social, cultural and physical components. Our values, interactions, behaviors, attitudes and feelings are included in its construction. Healthy constructions of sexuality prevent sexual violence. American culture, though, counters sexual violence prevention. Our country breeds sexual violence. The sexualized and demeaning language popularized in music, the sexual images on television and the associations between adolescent viewing patterns and their sexual activities are a testament to how society has failed the innocent. . . . We are socialized to believe women should be the object of a man's gaze. Any music video or television show or sitcom will maintain this idea. Women are prey.

Kayley Gillespie, "Portrayal of Women Perpetuates Dangerous Attitudes Toward Sexuality," *Oklahoma Daily*, March 29, 2012. http://oudaily.com.

victims with various weapons. In a study of more than fifty slasher films, Welsh found that although both men and women were victimized, men experienced a short, violent death while women were more likely to be stalked, tortured, and subjected to sexually laden violence in scenes of prolonged terror. Welsh found that "women in slasher films are also more likely to be featured in scenes involving sexual content. Specifically, female characters are far more likely to be featured as partially or fully naked, and, when sexual and violent images are concomitantly present, the film's antagonist is significantly more likely to attack a woman."[69]

Welsh also found that the violence against women was more likely to be voyeuristic and seen through the eyes of the slasher—having the viewer experience his point of view. Welsh speculates that such prolonged depictions of women in fear, partially clothed, and subjected to prolonged stalking may reinforce stereotypes of women as weak, helpless, and unable to fight back against an attacker. The stereotype, along with confusing the viewers' perceptions by mixing sexual arousal with violence, may influence vulnerable individuals into thinking that hurting women is enjoyable.

Female Revenge Films

While it is easy to despair over such negative depictions of women, movies also abound with powerful women who take revenge on their persecutor and triumph over him. One well-examined film is *The Girl with the Dragon Tattoo*, remade in the United States in 2011 after its original release in Sweden. In the film (which is based on the book by Stieg Larsson), the main character, Lisbeth Salandar, is sodomized and raped by her government-appointed guardian. As depicted, the scene is extremely uncomfortable to watch, and the audience develops a clear moral sympathy for Salandar, who is a victim of violence and an unfair governmental system that requires her to make monthly visits to the sadistic guardian. In the movie, however, Salandar is not a passive victim. She returns a second time, endures more violence, but this time is able to secretly tape the encounter. When she returns the third time, it is to turn the tables on her tormentor. She carves a crude tattoo on his torso that reads "I am a sadistic pig and rapist."[70] Clearly, the man will never again be able to take his clothes off in front of anyone without revealing, and supposedly being interrogated about, the tattoo. She also threatens to expose the man by uploading the tape to the media if he ever dares to retaliate against her or hurt her in any way.

In an article for the journal *Millions*, Emily Colette Wilkinson comments on why the sexual violence in this film might be cathartic rather than galling. She says:

For some, narrative art is also a means of gathering vicarious experience and coming to terms with our own experiences; it is a means of learning, in a safer way, about the world and human nature, especially its terrifying aspects. . . . From this intellectual position, watching unflinching portrayals of sexual violence can also be a way to guard against such evil in yourself, to identify it in others, to understand, in some small way, the horror that victims of sexual violence experience, and the damage that sexual violence inflicts on the lives and personalities of victims, their families, and their communities."[71]

Such positive effects of strong female characters can be seen in television as well. Christopher J. Ferguson deemed the effect the "Buffy Effect," after the once-popular television show *Buffy the Vampire Slayer.* Ferguson surveyed 150 university students after they had viewed a variety of TV shows that portrayed women responding in different ways to sexual violence. He found that the programs that had a submissive or weak female character rarely influenced the men's judgments overall about women, while the films that depicted a strong female lead influenced their reactions in positive ways. According to Ferguson: "Although sexual and violent content tends to get a lot of attention, I was surprised by how little impact such content had on attitudes toward women. Instead it seems to be portrayals of women themselves, positive or negative that have the most impact, irrespective of objectionable content. In focusing so much on violence and sex, we may have been focusing on the wrong things."[72]

"Watching unflinching portrayals of sexual violence can also be a way to guard against such evil in yourself, to identify it in others, to understand, in some small way, the horror that victims of sexual violence experience, and the damage that sexual violence inflicts on the lives and personalities of victims, their families, and their communities."[71]

— Film reviewer and writer Emily Colette Wilkinson.

Video Games

Another media genre that figures prominently in discussions of sexual violence is the video game. Some critics argue that even the plotlines of many video games start with a woman being victimized. Technology writer Ben Kuchera writes about how the murder of a hero's girlfriend or wife is sometimes used to propel video game story lines and provide the motive for the hero role: "It's . . . interesting how violence against women, or the early death of a female character, is so often used as a cheap emotional ploy in what amounts to a male power fantasy. Women get brutalized; we're upset because we lost something we care about: time to kill everything. It's effective and enjoyable. . . . After a while you just become numb to yet another woman getting shot in the head as a reason to shoot other people in the head."[73]

The violence Kuchera describes pales in comparison with some video game content. In the 2011 video game *Bulletstorm*, players are encouraged to shoot people in the private parts, with the effects being particularly gruesome and overly bloody. The dialogue makes fun of such violence and also makes reference to sex acts, incest, and venereal disease. The gruesomeness of such games prompted media psychiatrist Carole Lieberman to claim, "The increase in rapes can be attributed in large part to the playing out of [sexual] scenes in videogames."[74] While few researchers have dared to proclaim such a causal link, Lieberman seems unafraid to do so. She contends that "when videogames are violent and sexual, it causes the players to become desensitized to rape and think it is a 'game.'"[75] Lieberman's contentions are highly contested by others, who claim if there is such a link, it is certainly not one easily proved in the research.

A study by Karen Dill at Lenoir–Rhyne University in North Carolina found that short-term exposure to stereotypical sexualized images of women in video games made players more tolerant of real-life sexual harassment. She also found that long-term exposure to video game violence led to greater tolerance of sexual harassment and greater acceptance of the myth that women sometimes want to be raped. One video game explicitly depicts this myth. In *RapeLay* a player must use rape, bondage, and torture to win the game. Although it originated in Japan, it is widely available online in the United States. Dill explains the game's premise: "In the game, you follow a mother and her two daughters into a subway station and stalk and grope them. Along the way,

"Although sexual and violent content tends to get a lot of attention, I was surprised by how little impact such content had on attitudes toward women."[72]

— Texas A&M International University professor Christopher J. Ferguson.

Sexually Explicit Media and Real-World Sexual Behavior

In addition to the concern that sexual violence in the media may foster real-world sexual violence, many worry that sexual content of media in general will influence the sexual behaviors of young people. A 2013 study published in the *Journal of Sexual Medicine* may put some of these fears to rest. Gert Martin Hald and his colleagues at the University of Copenhagen in Denmark surveyed more than forty-five hundred people between the ages of fifteen and twenty-five. The researchers measured the youths' consumption of sexually explicit material from video games, television, magazines, and the Internet and also a variety of sexual behaviors, such as sex that involves the exchange of money. Hald and his team found that the consumption of sexually explicit media was only modestly correlated to sexual behavior, accounting for between 0.3 percent and 4 percent of differences in sexual behavior. According to Hald, this data suggests that other factors, such as sexual sensation seeking, may play a more important role in the sexual behaviors of teenagers and young adults.

your goal is to sexually arouse them, which takes time, as their initial reactions are fear and rejection. To succeed at the game, you rape women, which is depicted graphically, including how you score and advance in the game. You are able to impregnate women and abort their fetuses. The women and girls react to the repeated raping with fear and sorrow, though ultimately you can successfully make the women appear to like it." Dill argues that the game not only demeans women but also encourages sexual violence. "Research has shown that telling the story that women secretly enjoy rape encourages violence against women. Demeaning women, particularly sexually, encourages violence against women.

A game of this graphic nature teaches sexual violence, much like a violent game teaches and encourages aggression. It exposes players—among them children, since the game is available online—to explicit content. In rewarding rape and misogynistic behavior, it teaches and encourages those types of behaviors."[76]

A study published in 2010 lends some credence to Dill's conclusions. The study measured the short-term cognitive effects on male players of sexually explicit "female objectification" video games. It found that "playing a video game with the theme of female 'objectification' may prime thoughts related to sex, encourage men to view women as sex objects, and lead to self-reported tendencies to behave inappropriately towards women in social situations."[77]

Strong Female Leads Also Common

Games that encourage violence against women, or make it the point of the game, clearly have researchers worried about the effects of real-world violence against women. However, some video games feature strong and capable women characters. Some researchers believe this may provide an antidote to the others.

One of the most studied is the character of Lara Croft in the popular *Tomb Raider* games. While many feminist critics think Lara, like Barbie, is so well-endowed and curvy that her form is too ideal for women to emulate and makes boys see her as a sex object, others see Lara as a positive influence for boys and girls. Researchers like George Jones argue that boys who play this game are indirectly "accommodating shifting gender roles, building confidence that they can find even strong, challenging women attractive and that they won't be overwhelmed by their own fears as they deal with real girls. . . . These kids may approach their bad girls as objects at first, as the game or movie or the TV show begins to unfold, they are clearly identifying with them."[78]

Researcher Helen Kennedy finds that identification with a heroine who must take control of complex, scary, and often violent and threatening situations can be helpful for girls as well. "For the female game player," Kennedy writes, "these complex and visceral experiences may provide further opportunities for the gratification of fantasies of omnipotence."[79]

Sexual Violence in Music and Music Videos

Because male adolescents are by far the largest consumers of video games, many critics are most fearful that their attitudes are the ones being shaped by depictions of female characters. Like video games, many music videos and song lyrics are also replete with sexual imagery, especially the music that male adolescents find so appealing. Music videos, especially those that feature rap music, encourage sexual exploitation of women by showing women semiclad, sexually available, and enjoying being ogled while fully clothed male rap stars sing lyrics that describe women in derogatory sexual terms. Rap stars such as Drake in his song "Motto" speak of using women for sex, while Rick Ross in "You Isn't Even Know It" goes even further by suggesting date rape as a tactic for getting sex.

A 2011 video featuring the song "Monster" by Kanye West seemed to advocate that women do not even have to be alive to be sexualized. As blogger Lucy Jones describes it:

> The video starts with dead girls in sex-worker heels and underwear hanging from the ceiling with metal chains around their necks. They sway gently, presided over by Rick Ross in an armchair. Next, we see Kanye in bed with two negligee and suspender-clad beauties (also dead), rearranging their floppy limbs as they stare blankly. . . . Then, Jay-Z raps in front of a dead, naked model (with sexy heels) flung strangely across a sofa. It's not over: Kanye holds the garroted head of a woman by the hair, her severed hand bleeding nearby. And, in the next room, Rick Ross tucks into the stomach of a girl splayed across a counter. Erotic corpses.[80]

The images and lyrics seem almost unbelievably foul, yet many still argue that all artists push the limits of decency to shock and appall, and these widely popular rap stars are no different. As Brandon Soderberg writes in *Spin*: "'Monster' actually is an 'art piece' and 'as such' it takes more explication than a rap video really should. Kanye, the self-aware, sensitive rapper has crafted a surreal response to hip-hop misogyny [hatred of women] making the

Rappers Kanye West (left) and Jay-Z perform in 2011. A 2011 music video featuring both performers has been cited by some as an example of grossly derogatory and sexually exploitive work and by others as a provocative piece of art.

implicit violence of in-the-club videos, well, extremely explicit. Women tend to pose stoically in rap videos, so here they're frozen (thanks to rigor mortis) and dolled up without agency. It's a pitch-black comedy of rap-video excess."[81]

Yet others believe such content cannot be helping young men gain respect for women nor help young women's self-esteem. Activist Melinda Tankard Reist began a campaign protesting the video, contending that "the mainstreaming of videos like this increases desensitized and callous attitudes toward violence against women. . . . It feeds a growing appetite for sexual violence, witnessed or committed, that is inevitably acted out on victims of sex trafficking and rape. It teaches men that women are nothing more than bodies, raw meat, to be devoured."[82]

Changing Male Attitudes Toward Women

The argument over whether music, art, and literature have the power to affect people's attitudes and actions has been going on for centuries. But one recent study suggests that sexually explicit videos of women can, indeed, influence male attitudes. A 2012 study released by Melinda C.R. Burgess of Southwestern Oklahoma State University attempted to measure whether sexually explicit music videos would change college students' perception of rape. Burgess had 132 college students watch one of two music videos. One video was "These Boots Were Made for Walking" by Jessica Simpson, who covers her semiclad body in bubbles while washing a sports car. The video encourages the viewer to objectify Simpson as a purely sexual being. In the other video Faith Hill sings one of her signature songs about a romantic relationship. After watching the videos, all of the students were asked to read a hypothetical scenario about date rape and were asked to evaluate the responsibility of the rapist for the rape. The college students who viewed the Simpson video saw the rapist as less guilty of a crime than those who had watched the Hill video. The content of these videos is a lot tamer than much of the content of some of the most popular rap videos, heightening concerns about the level of influence more graphic music videos have on male attitudes toward women.

"The mainstreaming of videos like [Kanye West's music video 'Monster'] increases desensitized and callous attitudes toward violence against women."[82]

— Women's rights activist Melinda Tankard Reist.

No researcher can definitively proclaim that sexual violence in the media leads to the increased victimization of women in the real world. Yet it might be even harder to make a strong case for the view that such imagery is completely harmless.

Facts

- According to the American Academy of Child & Adolescent Psychiatry, the following themes in music lyrics may be detrimental to some teenagers: drugs and alcohol use that is glamorized, suicide as a solution to a problem, graphic violence, and sex that focuses on control, sadism, and similar issues.

- Many states have proposed laws that impose fines for retailers who sell music with Parental Advisory Labels to minors, although few of these laws are passed.

- Several studies have linked teenage exposure to sexual media to becoming sexually active at an earlier age.

- The popular Japanese games known as "hentai games" feature girlish-looking characters and are characterized by explicit sexual themes and images, sometimes featuring rape and bondage.

- Sexual content has been part of video games since they came into existence. In the 1982 Atari game *Custer's Revenge*, players controlled General George Custer, who had simulated sex with a naked Native American woman in captivity.

How Should the Problem of Media Violence Be Addressed?

Every few months news headlines seem to highlight an incident of a mass shooting. Whether at a school, theater, summer camp, or office, they seem to occur with nauseating regularity. Most incidents seem to involve disenchanted young men, mental illness, and even more commonly, one or several violent video games. While the causes of such tragedies are endlessly debated, calls for strict regulation and even bans of violent video games and other media are a constant feature of such debates.

In the United States, especially, cries to regulate any media bring objections on free speech grounds. Instead, the government has encouraged self-regulation in the form of rating systems, which video game, television, and moviemakers follow. Simultaneously, many observers instead put the blame on the parents of the shooters, suggesting that parents should be monitoring their children's media use, and perhaps more important, their mental states. What group of laws, regulations, and education of parents and children might help reduce the likelihood of these violent incidents is a subject of heated debate.

Regulation of the entertainment industry is not an easy option,

In the debate over regulation, where to draw the line on graphic depictions of violence is a complex issue. Should the same standard apply to violent shooter games such as Call of Duty *and movies such as the 1998 film* Saving Private Ryan *(pictured), which realistically depicts the horrors of war?*

as it raises questions about what should be regulated and what can be regulated in an open society with a long-standing commitment to free speech. Jonathan Gottschall questions whether curbing media violence is even possible: "This idea of blaming the media is an oldie and a baddy. First, practically, where would we draw the line? If we managed to ban trigger happy games like *Doom*, *Call of Duty*, and *Halo*, what would we do about violent films like *Saving Private Ryan* or equally gory classics like Homer's *Iliad*? Should we edit the kills out of Shakespeare's plays?"[83]

Gottschall places the blame for violent incidents on the shooters themselves and doubts that forms of regulation will stop them:

How should we respond to mass shooting tragedies? First we must resist the reflex to find and torch a scapegoat—whether in the entertainment industry or the gun lobby. Even if we could keep unstable people from consuming imaginary violence, they could still find plenty of inspiration from the nightly news, history, holy scripture, or their own fevered dreams. And even if we were able to pass laws that kept guns out of the hands of bad men (a tall order in a country with three hundred million guns in private circulation), how would we keep them from killing with improvised explosives or by plowing SUVs into dense crowds?[84]

Ratings

Despite such reasoning, various regulations and bans have been proposed and tried in the United States. For example, the video game industry maintains some of the most stringent rating systems of all media. The Entertainment Software Rating Board (ESRB) was founded in 1994 to oversee video game ratings. The Federal Communications Commission (FCC), for example, has praised the board as particularly effective. According to the industry, the ratings work. As ESRB president Patricia Vance says, "We have seen a fairly stable percentage of parents in terms of awareness and use in the last several years. . . . We're now at about 85% awareness among parents with kids who play video games, and 70 percent say they use them all the time or most of the time."[85]

Nevertheless, an FCC report found that video games rated "Mature" were being marketed to youth. The report found, for example, that underage youths could buy mature-rated video games 85 percent of the time, setting off concerns that further regulation was necessary. The Columbine school shooting in 1999 fostered a wave of public support for the regulation of violence in media, particularly video games. In the wake of the shootings, families of victims filed a $5 billion lawsuit against twenty-five entertainment and video companies, claiming that the video game *Doom* and other media violence incited the teen shooters. The case was never tried, however, as the courts found no scientific evidence for such a claim.

"Games are art. . . . Games should be afforded the same sort of protection and respect as other forms of speech."[86]

— Jason Della Rocca, program director of the International Game Developers Association.

Bans on Sales to Minors

Shortly thereafter, in 2003, Washington became the first state to regulate video games, specifically targeting the selling of games to

An M rating from the Entertainment Software Rating Board informs consumers that the game with this rating is not for children or young teens. Federal officials have praised the video game industry's rating system.

minors that feature violence against cops. It is one of the few states to successfully install such a ban. Critics of the Washington law include the program director of the International Game Developers Association, Jason Della Rocca: "Games are art. . . . Games should be afforded the same sort of protection and respect as other forms of speech."[86]

Other states that have tried such regulations have encountered firm opposition. In 2005 the California State Legislature passed AB 1179, which banned the sale of violent video games to anyone under age eighteen. The law also made mandatory the use of a more rigorous rating system than is currently used on video games. The law attached a maximum fine of $1,000 for each infraction.

California's ban on sales of violent video games to minors became law in October 2005. Before the law could go into effect, however, the Entertainment Merchants Association filed an appeal. The case made its way to the Supreme Court, which agreed to hear the case on First Amendment grounds. The court struck down the law, stating that it violated the First and Fourteenth Amendments: "Like the protected books, plays, and movies that preceded them, video games communicate ideas—and even social messages—through many familiar literary devices (such as characters, dialogue, plot, and music) and through features distinctive to the medium (such as the player's interaction with the virtual world). That suffices to confer First Amendment protection."[87]

Differing Views on Research

Though the Supreme Court is considered the final word in the American justice system, other states continue to attempt to restrict access to violent video games. A proposed law in Connecticut would prevent juveniles from playing violent video games in public places, such as arcades. The American Civil Liberties Union (ACLU) is leading opposition to the proposed bill, arguing that there is no proof that violent video games increase real-life violence. Though the ACLU has plenty of evidence for its view, the American public does not agree. A 2012 Harris poll found that 58 percent of American adults believe that violent video games cause real-life violence. Still, a direct causal relationship has been difficult to produce in a scientific setting. In response to public concerns, President Barack Obama announced a $500 million, twenty-three-point plan that directs the Centers for Disease Control and Prevention to conduct further research into the relationship between virtual violence and real-world violence.

Organizations such as the ACLU and the Media Coalition, organizations that defend the right to free speech, would argue that the government should save its money. In a review of research on the subject, the Media Coalition used several studies in its report, *Only a Game: Why Censoring New Media Won't Stop Gun Violence*. The coalition claims:

"Like the protected books, plays, and movies that preceded them, video games communicate ideas—and even social messages—through many familiar literary devices (such as characters, dialogue, plot, and music) and through features distinctive to the medium (such as the player's interaction with the virtual world). That suffices to confer First Amendment protection."[87]

— US Supreme Court, striking down a California law that would ban the sale of violent video games to players under eighteen.

- Crime statistics do not support the theory that new media causes violence.
- While media consumption has increased, violent crime rates in the U.S. have dropped, according to the government's National Crime Victimization Survey.
- In national populations, including the U.S., more video game sales correlate with less crime, according to a 2012 Washington Post review of the 10 biggest video game markets around the world.
- Profiles of mass shooters by the FBI and the Secret Service do not list an attraction to violent video games as a contributing or significant factor.[88]

In addition, the coalition found research into violence as inconclusive and unable to meet the criteria of reproducible results. As a result, the coalition concluded that "a majority of Americans may believe that fictional violence leads to violence in real life. But common sense and objective research does not show it."[89]

Many commentators do not agree with these conclusions and say that they defy common sense, since almost all of the mass shooters in recent years have also been avid gamers. These people argue that society prohibits other media that it considers unsuitable for children—including, for example, pornography and obscenity, though no studies prove conclusively that pornography harms young people.

In the absence of laws that meet the constitutional test, entertainment industry rating systems have gained in importance. For many state and local governments, restrictions on young people's access to violent media hinge on these self-imposed labeling systems that identify content inappropriate for children.

Movie Restrictions

The effectiveness of ratings is often disputed. Many say rating systems are seriously flawed and lack objectivity and consistency. Moviemakers, for example, dread having an NC-17 rating on their movies because it means one of the largest groups of movie-

"Crime statistics do not support the theory that new media causes violence."[88]

— Media Coalition, an organization that defends the right to free speech.

Parental Controls

According to the American Academy of Child & Adolescent Psychiatry, parents can minimize the potential effects of television violence in these ways:

- pay attention to the programs their children are watching and watch some with them
- set limits on the amount of time they spend with the television; consider removing the TV set from the child's bedroom
- point out that although the actor has not actually been hurt or killed, such violence in real life results in pain or death
- refuse to let the children see shows known to be violent, and change the channel or turn off the TV set when offensive material comes on, with an explanation of what is wrong with the program
- disapprove of the violent episodes in front of the children, stressing the belief that such behavior is not the best way to resolve a problem
- to offset peer pressure among friends and classmates, contact other parents and agree to enforce similar rules about the length of time and type of program the children may watch

American Academy of Child & Adolescent Psychiatry, "Children and TV Violence," March 2011. www.aacap.org.

goers—teenagers under the age of seventeen—cannot attend the films. But with enough bullying, the Motion Picture Association of America (MPAA) frequently reviews and changes such ratings. Another common complaint is that there is no consistency in establishing R-rated films. In 2007, for example, *Hostel: Part 2*, a graphic horror movie that includes scenes of decapitation and cannibalism, deservedly, it seems, received an R rating. Yet the film *Once*, about two singers who fall in love, also received an R rating, for language. More recently, a documentary called *Bully*, released in 2012 and showing graphic incidents of bullying, received an R rating because of language. Yet the entire point was to show the harm that bullying does. The producers hoped that many teenagers would see the film and come away with a deeper understanding of the lifelong effects of bullying.

Some argue that these inconsistencies could be remedied with further regulation and without letting the movie industry regulate itself. Some observers have proposed that the government regulate movies or make ratings simpler by not using context to come up with a rating. For example, instead of judging whether the violence or language is acceptable because of the nature of the situation, Adam Gittlel, author of the blog *REEL CHANGE*, has proposed that movies get an automatic NC-17 rating if they depict a murder, cruelty to animals or humans, or sexual violence such as rape. In response to such critics, the MPAA announced in July 2013 that it would beef up its rating system. Called the "Check the Box" campaign, theaters will now have more information about individual movies and why they carry a particular rating. A film that carries a PG-13 or R rating, for example, will now be accompanied by text that explains the rationale for the code—for example, whether the rating resulted from profanity, nudity, smoking, drug use, or violence. One recent PG film carried this description: "Rated PG for fantasy action violence, some scary images and mild language."[90]

As flawed as the system is, however, many parents defend it on the grounds that it is the only guide they have to keep track of what movies their kids wish to see. In addition, when a film receives an R rating, many parents decide to see the film anyway with their teenager, resulting in meaningful discussions about the film and further keeping the parents abreast of their teen's viewing habits.

Television

Even though television started carrying similar ratings to films to help parents regulate content in the home, Congress supported technological solutions to give parents better control. In 2008 Congress passed the Child Safe Viewing Act to study advanced blocking technologies that are available for each kind of media, resulting in the V-Chip. Since 2000, most televisions have a built in V-Chip that allows parents to block programs they do not want their children to view. The V-Chip may have questionable value, however. Some parents have difficulty understanding how to use it. Perhaps even more important, the addition of hundreds of viewing opportunities, including the use of on-demand technologies, makes sifting through all of the programming options an almost impossible task.

Parents face such challenges as television has become increasingly violent and sexual, depicting acts that would have been unacceptable even five years ago. Producers of some of the most popular shows on television, including *Dexter, The Walking Dead,* and *Game of Thrones*, take pride in the movie-like violence and sex depicted in their programs. *Los Angeles Times* reporter Scott Collins points out that the large audiences such shows garner translate into a large "go ahead" to the movie networks:

> Although viewers sometimes complain about violence, they tend to get more irked by raw language or sexuality. Often they rationalize violence as long as it's familiar to a genre, such as horror, or has a moralistic message attached. [TV historian Tim] Brooks recalls a focus group 20 years ago when he worked for USA Network. Some parents talked about how much they liked the show "Walker, Texas Ranger," which featured Chuck Norris as a crime fighter who took out the bad guys with martial-arts moves.
>
> When the moderator pointed out that research had determined "Walker" was one of the most violent shows on TV, the room fell silent. Then one woman piped up and said that might be true, but it was OK because Norris played a good guy who helped people in trouble.[91]

"Although viewers sometimes complain about violence, they tend to get more irked by raw language or sexuality. Often they rationalize violence as long as it's familiar to a genre, such as horror, or has a moralistic message attached."[91]

— *Los Angeles Times* reporter Scott Collins.

As with movies, games, and music videos, graphic violence on television has also increased in recent years. Popular shows such as The Walking Dead *(pictured) strive to present realistic depictions of violence and sex.*

Such acceptance does not translate to sexual content, however. Many still recall the "wardrobe mishap" Janet Jackson had during live coverage of the Super Bowl in 2004, when her nipple was exposed on camera. The incident was talked about for weeks as shocking. Such discrepancies on what viewers find acceptable, critics argue, would make it difficult to come up with a single rating system that everyone could agree on.

Music Restrictions

The Recording Industry Association of America represents the recording industry and administers the Parental Advisory Label program, which labels music that contains explicit lyrics, including violent and/or sexual content. The label is supposed to allow parents to readily censor which music their children choose. While parental advisory labels may be well intentioned, critics argue that these labels do too little to keep explicit material away from young people. Many say the music industry markets music with objectionable lyrics to those under eighteen. In addition, online sites that offer music and music videos have not adopted the rating system, and, since most music is purchased online, a new way to regulate music is necessary.

Teaching Media Literacy

With every regulatory method under attack as not thorough enough, some observers say that the most effective way to regulate media violence is by encouraging media literacy. In the digital age, when music, video games, and films are a few computer keyboard clicks away, education and critical thinking may be the key to helping young people contend with or steer clear of media violence.

According to David S. Bickham, the creation of successful media literacy programs is key: "Educational interventions based around teaching children to analyze and question media can dramatically reduce the effects of violent media. Children who learn critical thinking skills are equipped to recognize the falsities presented in violent media. When coupled with strategies to reduce their overall exposure, these techniques are particularly successful."[92]

The online organization LimiTV gives several concrete examples of how parents can help children and adolescents become savvier about the way media depicts topics. Parents can ask adolescents to think about how the media portrays young people. The organization quotes from studies that show that teens are often depicted as "kids in crisis," using as proof an excerpt from *Fateful Choices*, a report from the Carnegie Council on Adolescent Development published in 1992. "The state of adolescent health in America has reached crisis proportions," the authors write. "Large numbers of ten-to-fifteen year olds suffer from depression that may lead to suicide; they jeopardize their future by abusing illegal drugs and alcohol, and by smoking; they engage in premature, unprotected sexual activity; they are victims or perpetrators of violence. . . . By age 15, about a quarter of all young adolescents are engaged in behaviors that are harmful to themselves and others."[93]

"Educational interventions based around teaching children to analyze and question media can dramatically reduce the effects of violent media. Children who learn critical thinking skills are equipped to recognize the falsities presented in violent media."[92]

— Media expert David S. Bickham.

"A Safe Escape from Modern Problems"

Los Angeles Times film critic Betsy Sharkey believes efforts to regulate movie violence are misguided. She disputes the view that movies are to blame for real-world violence.

What possible good can come from any depiction of the horrific on screen?

Let's start with the obvious. A good deal of movie violence is designed as a way for us to experience it vicariously. Whether the topic is war, high-flying superheroes, cops and robbers, comedy or Freddy Krueger—films are packed with plots whose main purpose is to deliver payback.

That is why "Taken" had such mass appeal. It was easy to empathize with Liam Neeson's desperate father, his anguish when his daughter is kidnapped by ruthless international sex slavers. It was easier still to forgive the brutal swath he cut getting her back. Take that raw revenge and put a superpower at the other end of the barrel and you find a steady stream of good guys with guns we want in our camp—Bourne, Bond, the Terminator, Transformers, G.I. Joe.

For the vast majority of moviegoers, fantasy, fairy tales, the hyper-realized worlds of comic books, even the darkest of parables, offer a safe escape from modern problems—not an excuse to create more. . . . It's exhilarating to watch Peter Parker scale buildings, Clark Kent leap them, Batman zoom around them. Even as the buildings crumble and the bodies of their adversaries pile up, the consistent take-away is that there are repercussions for breaking the rules.

Betsy Sharkey, "Critic's Notebook: Movie Violence Must Not Be Stopped," *Los Angeles Times*, February 15, 2013. www.latimes.com.

If parents were to ask teenagers if this depiction was accurate, the teens could, for example, research how many teens fit this description and whether the media reporting is exaggerated. LimiTV suggests questions such as these:

> According to the Carnegie report, only 25% of young people in the United States could accurately be described as "in crisis." Media literacy, then, would raise the following questions about the media's depiction of young people: What about the other 75%? Where are their stories being told? Why are the news and entertainment media focused on young people in trouble? How does the skewed depiction of "kids in crisis" shape teens' perceptions of themselves? How does it shape policies implemented by adults?[94]

LimiTV argues that media literacy has proved to be an effective way to help teens manage media. One study, for example, shows that "third-graders who received media literacy training related to alcohol ads were less likely to rate the ads positively, were less attracted to alcohol promotional material, and showed greater disdain for alcohol commercials."[95]

Learning to Think Critically

While parents can help children understand the viewpoint behind the media, pilot curriculum is also being tested in schools to improve children's ability to think critically about what they watch on television and in movies. In 2005 curriculum called "Beyond Blame: Challenging Violence in the Media" was used in three inner-city middle schools in which all participants were Hispanic. Teens were asked to evaluate violent television programs and were asked questions about the content. According to researchers Theresa Webb and others, who developed the curriculum: "Three of 24 questions were open-ended (What usually happens in a television show or movie when someone gets angry? What is the cycle of violence? What can be done so that TV shows and movies focus more on peaceful, nonviolent solutions to problems?)."[96]

Other multiple-choice questions targeted students' attitudes and beliefs. An example of a belief students were queried about is,

"In general, it is wrong to hit other people."[97] In response, students were asked to choose from one of four responses: It's perfectly okay, It's sort of okay, It's sort of wrong, or It's really wrong. The teens were asked to fill out a questionnaire both before and after the program that queried them about their awareness of violence in the media. Teens were overwhelmingly more aware of the way the media portrayed violence after the program.

Such strategies could make young people more discerning consumers of information, laying a foundation for a lifelong ability to question what they view and hear. One thing seems clear: Exposure to violent images and music is ever expanding as consumers have more access to a wide range of material on the Internet. Understanding how this and other media influences society's behavior and attitudes may be a crucial part of dealing with the problems of real-life violence.

Facts

- In January 2013 Vice President Joe Biden was assigned to lead a special committee to examine ways of curtailing gun violence. As part of the study, the group will examine the effects of violent media on young people.

- In 2003 the ESRB introduced new rating descriptors for the violence in a video game, including cartoon violence, intense violence, sexual violence, and fantasy violence.

- In May 2013 the son of evangelist Billy Graham, Franklin Graham, proposed that violent entertainment media should be subjected to a special tax. The tax proceeds would be used to help the victims of gun violence.

Source Notes

Introduction: Media Violence Versus Real Violence

1. Christopher Nolan, director, *The Dark Knight Rises*, Warner Brothers, 2008.
2. Quoted in Eddie Makuch, "CT Senator Talks Role of Violent Games in Mass Shootings," Gamespot, June 25, 2013. www.gamespot.com.
3. William Saletan, "Mental Illness Is Common Thread in Mass Shootings," *Buffalo (NY) News*, April 7, 2013. www.buffalonews.com.
4. Dottie Pacharis, "Gun Control Is Not the Answer to Mass Shootings. Mental Health Treatment Is," *Guardian* (London), June 22, 2013. www.guardian.co.uk.
5. Dennis Scimeca, "I'm Mentally Ill, I Love Violent Video Games, and They've Never Made Me Feel Like Killing Anyone," Kotaku, January 16, 2013. http://kotaku.com.
6. Scimeca, "I'm Mentally Ill."

Chapter One: What Are the Origins of the Media Violence Debate?

7. Henry Jenkins, "A Few Thoughts on Media Violence . . . ," *Official Weblog of Henry Jenkins*, April 25, 2007. http://henryjenkins.org.
8. Steven J. Kirsh, *Children, Adolescents, and Media Violence: A Critical Look at the Research*. Thousand Oaks, CA: Sage, 2006, p. 6.
9. Kirsh, *Children, Adolescents, and Media Violence*, p. 6.
10. Quoted in Garth S. Jowett et al., *Children and the Movies: Media Influence and the Payne Fund Controversy*. New York: Cambridge University Press, 1996, p. 337.
11. The Motion Picture Production Code, "The Production Code of the Motion Picture Industry." http://productioncode.dhwritings.com.
12. The Motion Picture Production Code, "The Production Code of the Motion Picture Industry."
13. Eugene V. Beresin, "The Impact of Media Violence on Children and Adolescents: Opportunities for Clinical Interventions," American Academy of Child & Adolescent Psychiatry, 2010. www.aacap.org.
14. Beresin, "The Impact of Media Violence on Children and Adolescents."
15. David Trend, *The Myth of Media Violence: A Critical Introduction*. Malden, MA: Blackwell, 2007, p. 3.
16. Greg Braxton, "Extreme Violence Cuts Bloody Path Through Noteworthy TV Dramas," *Los Angeles Times*, November 10, 2011. http://articles.latimes.com.
17. American Academy of Pediatrics, "Joint Statement on the Impact of Entertainment Violence on Children," July 26, 2000. www.2aap.org.
18. Media Violence Commission, "Report of the Media Violence Commission," *Aggressive Behavior*, 2012. http://onlinelibrary.wiley.com.
19. Jonathan Gottschall, "2013: What *Should* We Be Worried About?," *Edge*, 2013, www.edge.org.
20. Quoted in Jason Schreier, "From Halo to Hot Sauce: What 25 Years of Violent Video Game Research Looks Like," Kotaku, January 17, 2013. http://kotaku.com.

21. Peggy Noonan, "Newtown," *WSJ Blogs, Wall Street Journal*, December 17, 2012. http://blogs.wsj.com.

22. Quoted in Stephen Dinan, "Critics of Violent Films, Video Games Note the Call for Study, Not Controls," *Washington Times*, January 16, 2013. www.washingtontimes.com.

Chapter Two: Does Violent Media Cause Violent Behavior?

23. Quoted in Helen Pidd, "Anders Breivik 'Trained' for Shooting Attacks by Playing Call of Duty," *Guardian* (London), April 19, 2012. http://guardian.co.uk.

24. Quoted in Pidd, "Anders Breivik 'Trained' for Shooting Attacks by Playing Call of Duty."

25. Marjorie Heins, "Violence and the Media," First Amendment Center, 2001. www.freedomforum.org.

26. Heins, "Violence and the Media."

27. Malte Elson, "Media Violence and Criminal Behavior," *Things We Don't Know* (blog), June 19, 2013. http://blog.thingswedon'tknow.com.

28. Heins, "Violence and the Media."

29. David S. Bickham, testimony before the US Senate Committee on the Judiciary, March 29, 2006. www.judiciary.senate.gov.

30. Quoted in Patricia Sullivan, "Leonard D. Eron, 87; Linked TV Content to Aggression and Destructive Behavior," *Washington Post*, May 21, 2007. www.washingtonpost.com.

31. Maren Strenziok et al., "Fronto-Parietal Regulation of Media Violence Exposure in Adolescents: A Multi-Method Study," *Social Cognitive and Affective Neuroscience*, 2010. http://scan.oxfordjournals.org.

32. Media Violence Commission, "Report of the Media Violence Commission."

33. Quoted in Sasha Emmons, "Kids and Violence in Media," Parenting.com. www.parenting.com.

34. Quoted in Emmons, "Kids and Violence in Media."

35. Bickham, testimony.

36. Quoted in Alexa Ray Corriea, "University Study Says Media Consumption Not a Predictor of Violent Behavior," *Polygon*, May 22, 2013. www.polygon.com.

37. Quoted in Corriea, "University Study Says Media Consumption Not a Predictor of Violent Behavior."

38. Paul Waldman, "Media Violence Versus Real Violence," *American Prospect*, January 11, 2013. http://prospect.org.

39. Gottschall, "2013: What *Should* We Be Worried About?"

40. Free Expression Policy Project, "Fact Sheets: Media Violence," July 2011. www.fepproject.org.

41. Institute of Medicine, "Priorities for Research to Reduce the Threat of Firearm-Related Violence," June 2013. www.iom.edu.

Chapter Three: Are Violent Video Games Harming Youth?

42. Tadhg Kelly, "All Games Are (in a Sense) Violent," Techcrunch.com, December 22, 2012. http://techcrunch.com.

43. Quoted in Schreier, "From Halo to Hot Sauce."

44. Douglas Gentile and Craig Anderson, "Don't Read More Into the Supreme Court's Ruling on the California Video Game Law," Newswise, June 30, 2011. www.newswise.com.

45. L. Rowell Huesmann, "Nailing the Coffin Shut on Doubts That Violent Video Games Stimulate Aggression: Comment on Anderson et al. (2010)," *Psychological Bulletin*, American Psychological Association, March 2010. www.apa.org.

46. L. Rowell Huesmann et al., "The Effects of Playing Violent Video Games on Youth: A Three-Year Longitudinal Study," University of Michigan Institute for Social Research, 2011. http://rcgd.isr.umich.edu.

47. Quoted in ScienceDaily, "Violent Video Games Are a Risk Factor for Criminal Behavior and Aggression, New Evidence Shows," March 26, 2013. www.sciencedaily.com.

48. Quoted in ScienceDaily, "Violent Video Games Are a Risk Factor for Criminal Behavior and Aggression, New Evidence Shows."

49. Media Smarts, "Violence—Overview," 2011. http://mediasmarts.ca.

50. Quoted in Media Smarts, "Violence—Overview."

51. Jenny McCartney, "There Is a Majority Against Vile Video Games, and It Is Moral," *Telegraph* (London), March 30, 2008. www.telegraph.co.uk.

52. Schreier, "From Halo to Hot Sauce."

53. Quoted in Schreier, "From Halo to Hot Sauce."

54. Quoted in Schreier, "From Halo to Hot Sauce."

55. Christopher J. Ferguson, "Video Games Don't Make Kids Violent," *Time*, December 7, 2011. http://ideas.time.com.

56. Ferguson, "Video Games Don't Make Kids Violent."

57. Kelly, "All Games Are (in a Sense) Violent."

58. Quoted in Cheryl K. Olson, "Children's Motivations for Video Game Play in the Context of Normal Development," *Review of General Psychology*, 2010. www.apa.org.

59. Quoted in Olson, "Children's Motivations for Video Game Play in the Context of Normal Development."

60. Olson, "Children's Motivations for Video Game Play in the Context of Normal Development."

61. Quoted in Ivan Boothe, "5 Reasons Targeting 'Violence in the Media' Won't Help Heal Our Society," Fellowship of Reconciliation, April 9, 2013. http://forusa.org.

62. Quoted in Cheryl K. Olson, "It's Perverse, but It's Also Pretend," *New York Times*, June 27, 2011. www.nytimes.com.

63. Matt Peckham, "Guns, Violence, Video Games, Irrationalism and the NRA's Tedious New iOS App," *Time*, January 15, 2013. http://techland.time.com.

Chapter Four: What Is the Impact of Sexual Violence in the Media?

64. Parents Television Council, "Women in Peril: A Look at TV's Disturbing New Storyline Trend," October 2009. www.parentstv.org.

65. Parents Television Council, "Women in Peril."

66. Neil M. Malamuth, "Do Sexually Violent Media Indirectly Contribute to Antisocial Behavior?," paper prepared for Surgeon General's Workshop on Pornography and Public Health, June 22–24, 1986. www.sscnet.ucla.edu.

67. Malamuth, "Do Sexually Violent Media Indirectly Contribute to Antisocial Behavior?"

68. Quoted in Kerby Anderson, "Sex and Violence on Television," Probe Ministries. www.probe.org.

69. Andrew Welsh, "Sex and Violence in the Slasher Horror Film," *Journal of Criminal Justice and Popular Culture*, 2009. www.albany.edu.

70. *The Girl with the Dragon Tattoo*, directed by David Fincher, Columbia Pictures, 2011.

71. Emily Colette Wilkinson, "Can Sexual Violence in Movies Be Edifying? From Straw Dogs to the Girl with the Dragon Tattoo," *Millions*, September 23, 2011. www.themillions.com.

72. Quoted in Michelle Castillo, "TV's 'Buffy Effect' Seen to Impact Views on Women," CBS News, August 31, 2013. www.cbsnews.com.

73. Ben Kuchera, "The Use of Violence Against Women to Justify, and Propel, the Stories of Modern Video Games," *Penny Arcade Report*, May 30, 2013. www.penny-arcade.com.

74. Quoted in John Brandon, "Is Bulletstorm the Worst Video Game in the World?," FoxNews.com, February 8, 2011. www.foxnews.com.

75. Quoted in Jason Schreier, "Playing the Rape Card: 'Media Psychiatrist' Ratchets Up Anti-Videogame Rhetoric," *Wired*, February 11, 2011. www.wired.com.

76. Karen Dill, "Making a (Video) Game out of Rape," *Psychology Today*, March 30, 2010. www.psychologytoday.com.

77. Mike Z. Yao et al., "Sexual Priming, Gender Stereotyping, and Likelihood to Sexually Harass: Examining the Cognitive Effects of Playing a Sexually-Explicit Video Game," *Sex Roles*, 2010. www.springer.com.

78. Quoted in Helen W. Kennedy, "Lara Croft: Feminist Icon or Cyberbimbo? On the Limits of Textual Analysis," *International Journal of Computer Game Research*, December 2002. www.gamestudies.org.

79. Kennedy, "Lara Croft."

80. Lucy Jones, "Music Video for Monster Features Sexualised Violence. Way to go, Kanye!," *Telegraph* (London), December 30, 2010. http://blogs.telegraph.co.uk.

81. Brandon Soderberg, "In Defense of Kanye West's 'Monster,'" *Spin*, June 18, 2011. www.spin.com.

82. Melinda Tankard Reist, "Tell Universal Music and Kanye West Eroticized Violence Against Women Is Unacceptable," Petition, July 2011. www.change.org.

Chapter Five: How Should the Problem of Media Violence Be Addressed?

83. Gottschall, "2013: What *Should* We Be Worried About?"

84. Gottschall, "2013: What *Should* We Be Worried About?"

85. Quoted in Anthony John Agnello, "The ESRB Ratings Work: 85% of Parents Understand System," *Digital Trends*, February 14, 2013. www.digitaltrends.com.

86. Quoted in Chris Morris, "Washington Bans 'Violent' Game Sales," CNN Money, May 21, 2003. http://money.cnn.com.

87. Quoted in John D. Sutter, "Supreme Court Sees Video Games as Art," CNN Tech, June 27, 2011. www.cnn.com.

88. Media Coalition, "Only a Game: Why Censoring New Media Won't Stop Gun Violence," 2013. http://mediacoalition.org.

89. Media Coalition, "Only a Game."

90. FilmRatings.com, "The Film Rating System." www.filmratings.com.

91. Scott Collins, "Acceptable Level of TV Violence Is Ever Shifting for Viewers, Execs," *Los Angeles Times*, February 15, 2013. www.latimes.com.

92. Bickham, testimony.

93. Carnegie Council on Adolescent Development, *Fateful Choices: Healthy Youth for the 21st Century*, 1992. http://carnegie.org.

94. LimiTV, "Media Literacy," www.limitv.org.

95. LimiTV, "Media Literacy."

96. Theresa Webb et al., "Media Literacy as a Violence-Prevention Strategy: A Pilot Evaluation," *Health Promotion Practice*, 2009. www.sophe.org.

97. Webb et al., "Media Literacy as a Violence-Prevention Strategy: A Pilot Evaluation."

Related Organizations and Websites

American Civil Liberties Union (ACLU)

125 Broad St.
New York, NY 10004
phone: (212) 549-2627
website: www.aclu.org

The American Civil Liberties Union seeks to defend the constitutional rights to free speech for all Americans. The ACLU opposes censorship of all forms of speech, including governmental regulation of the media and media violence. The organization produces many public policy reports and other publications on a variety of issues related to free speech, including media violence.

American Psychological Association (APA)

750 First St. NE
Washington, DC
phone: (800) 374-2721
e-mail: publicaffairs@apa.org
website: www.apa.org

The American Psychological Association is a society of psychologists that promotes the field of psychology, producing a number of reports, articles, educational resources, and press releases concerning violence in the media and how it affects youth. The APA supports public policies that reduce violent content of video games and other media.

Canadians Concerned About Violence in Entertainment

167 Glen Rd.
Toronto, ON M4W 2W8
e-mail: info@c-cave.com
website: www.c-cave.com

Canadians Concerned About Violence in Entertainment works to educate the public about how media violence impacts society. To this end, the organization promotes media literacy programs to inform consumers about the effects of violent media and also governmental regulation of the entertainment industry.

Cato Institute

1000 Massachusetts Ave. NW
Washington, DC 20001-5403
phone: (202) 842-0200
website: www.cato

The Cato Institute is a libertarian public policy research foundation that seeks to promote the principles of individual liberty and limited government. To this end, the institute opposes governmental regulation of all media, including violent media. It publishes a variety of educational materials related to public policy, including the *Cato Policy Analysis* and *Cato Policy Review*.

Center for Media Literacy (CML)

23852 Pacific Coast Hwy.
Malibu, CA 90265
phone: (310) 456-1225
e-mail: cml@medialit.org
website: www.medialit.org

The Center for Media Literacy seeks to promote media literacy to empower individuals to make informed choices about how they consume media. To this end, the CML publishes a variety of educational materials and the newsletter *CONNECTIONS*.

Center on Media and Child Health

300 Longwood Ave.
Boston, MA 02115
phone: (617) 355-2000
website: www.cmch.tv

The Center on Media and Child Health at Children's Hospital Boston, Harvard Medical School, and Harvard School of Public Health is dedicated to understanding the effects of media on the physical and mental health of children. As such, the center conducts and provides evidence-based research to programs that address children's interactions with media.

Common Sense Media (CSM)

650 Townsend, Suite 435
San Francisco, CA 94103
phone: (415) 863-0600
website: www.commonsensemedia.org

Common Sense Media is a nonprofit organization that advocates on a variety of issues that affect children and families. The organization seeks to provide trustworthy information so that families can make informed choices about what media they consume. The CSM publishes a variety of educational materials, including reports on the effects that violent media have on young users.

Entertainment Software Ratings Board (ESRB)

317 Madison Ave., 22nd Floor
New York, NY 10017

The Entertainment Software Ratings Board is the self-regulating body for the computer and video gaming industry. The ESRB was formed in 1994 to aid gamers and their families in making informed choices about which games to purchase. The board's functions include determining content-based ratings and enforcing advertising guidelines.

Federal Communications Commission (FCC)

445 Twelfth St. SW
Washington, DC 20554
phone: (888) 225-5322
e-mail: fccinfor@fcc.gov
website: www.fcc.gov

The Federal Communications Commission is a governmental agency that regulates telecommunications within the United States. The FCC creates and implements policies for communication via television, radio, satellite, and cable. A variety of reports and educational materials are available on the commission's website.

International Game Developers Association

19 Mantua Rd.
Mt. Royal, NJ 08061
phone: (856) 423-2990
website: www.igda.org

The International Game Developers Association is an independent, nonprofit organization for game developers. The association promotes the professional development of individuals who create video games and advocates for anti-censorship laws and other issues that affect the development of games.

National Cable and Telecommunications Association

25 Massachusetts Ave. NW, Suite 100
Washington, DC 20001
phone: (202) 222-2300
website: www.ncta.com

The National Cable and Telecommunications Association is the foremost trade association of the cable industry. The association works with Congress, the courts, and the public to address issues, including media violence, that affect the industry and the American public.

Parents Television Council

707 Wilshire Blvd., Suite 2075
Los Angeles, CA 90017
phone: (213) 403-1300
e-mail: editor@parentstb.org
website: www.parentstv.org

The Parents Television Council promotes responsible, family-friendly television programming. The organization publishes the *Family Guide to Prime Time Television*, which provides detailed information about the content of sitcoms and other television broadcasts. It also publishes current television and movie reviews so that consumers can make informed choices about the media they consume.

Additional Reading

Books

Gayle Brewer, ed., *Media Psychology*. New York: Palgrave Macmillan, 2011.

Dave Cullen, *Columbine*. New York: Twelve, 2009.

Christopher J. Ferguson, *Adolescents, Crime, and the Media: A Critical Analysis*. New York: Springer, 2013.

Dave Grossman, *On Killing: The Psychological Cost of Learning to Kill in War and Society*. New York: Back Bay, 2009.

Steffen Hantke, *The American Horror Film: The Genre at the Turn of the Millennium*. Jackson: Mississippi University Press, 2010.

Steven J. Kirsh, *Children, Adolescents, and Media Violence: A Critical Look at the Research*. 2nd ed., Thousand Oaks, CA: Sage, 2012.

Lawrence Kutner and Cheryl K. Olson, *Grand Theft Childhood: The Surprising Truth About Violent Video Games*. New York: Simon & Schuster, 2011.

Peter Langman, *Why Kids Kill: Inside the Minds of School Shooters*. New York: Palgrave Macmillan, 2010.

Marcel Lebrun, *Books, Blackboards, and Bullets: School Shootings and Violence in America*. Lanham, MD: Rowman & Littlefield Education, 2009.

Jane McGonigal, *Reality Is Broken: Why Games Make Us Better and How They Can Change the World*. New York: Penguin, 2011.

Steven Pinker, *The Better Angels of Our Nature: Why Violence Has Declined*. New York: Penguin, 2012.

Victor C. Strasburger, Barbara J. Wilson, and Amy B. Jordan, *Children, Adolescents, and the Media*. 3rd ed. Thousand Oaks, CA: Sage, 2014.

Gwyn Symonds, *The Aesthetics of Violence in Contemporary Media*. London: Continuum, 2012.

Periodicals and Internet Sources

American Academy of Child & Adolescent Psychiatry, "Children and Video Games: Playing with Violence," March 2011. www.aacap.org.

Benedict Carey, "Shooting in the Dark," *New York Times*, February 11, 2013.

Common Sense Media, "10 Most Violent Video Games (and 10 Plus Alternatives)," *Huffington Post*, June 24, 2013.

Roger Ebert, "Getting Real About Movie Ratings," *Wall Street Journal*, December 11, 2010.

Sasha Emmons, "Is Media Violence Damaging to Kids?," CNN, February 21, 2013.

Erik Kain, "The Truth About Video Games and Gun Violence," *Mother Jones*, June 11, 2013.

Patrick Markey, "In Defense of Violent Video Games," *U.S. News & World Report*, April 29, 2013.

Roger Simon, "Supreme Court Says Violence Ok. Sex? Maybe," Politico.com, June 28, 2011. www.politico.com.

Robby Soave, "Study: Violent Video Games Do Not Cause Real Violence," *Daily Caller*, May 23, 2013.

Maia Szalavitz, "Violent Video Games Don't Make Us Less Caring," *Time*, July 8, 2013.

Adam Thierer, "Should We Regulate Violent TV?," *City Journal*, Autumn 2011.

Index

Connecticut, 6, 9, 73
  See also Lanza, Adam
court rulings, 41, 53, 72–73
Croft, Lara (fictional character), 64
culprit mentality, 26
culture, violence has always been part of, 12–13, 70

Danse Macabre (King), 38
DeLisi, Matt, 46–47
Della Rocca, Jason, 72
desensitization to violence
  of children, 23
  described, 12
  as effect of media violence, 31
  MRI studies on, 35
  against women, 58, 62
Dill, Karen, 62–63
disruptive behavior disorders, 34
Donnerstein, Edward, 58
Drake, 65

Elson, Malte, 31
Entertainment Merchants Association, 72–73
Entertainment Software Rating Board (ESRB), 71, **72**, 82
environment as factor in violence, 27, 37
Eron, Leonard D., 33–35

Fateful Choices (Carnegie Council on Adolescent
    Development), 79
fears of world, unrealistic
  described, 12
  research on, 23–24, 31, 40, 41
Federal Communications Commission (FCC), 71
female victimization/objectification
  hentai games and, 68
  increase in, on television, 55
  in music lyrics and video, 65–67
  in video games, 64
  See also sexual violence and women
Ferguson, Christopher J., 37, 49, 52–53, 61
firearm violence, research on, 40
First Amendment rights, 53, 54, 69, 72–73
Fourteenth Amendment rights, 73
Free Expression Policy Project, 39, 41
free speech rights, 53, 54, 69, 72–73
functional violence, 42–43

Garrison, Michelle, 36
gender
  and effect of television on children, 21
  and effect of video games
    on impulsive behavior, 54
    as release for aggressive feelings, 51–52
    on sexual violence against women, 61–64
    with strong women characters, 64
    on youth, 54
  and effect of violent movies, 17, 60, 61
  media focus on, 52–53
genetics as factor in violence, 27, 37
Gentile, Doug, 26, 43–44
Gillespie, Kayley, 59
Girl with a Dragon Tattoo (movie), 60–61
Gittlel, Adam, 76

God of War (video game), 42–43
Gottschall, Jonathan
  on media violence
    in classics, 70
    and inconclusive evidence, 25
  on positive aspects of adventure style video games, 44
  on public response to mass shootings, 70–71
  on role of violence in moral code, 38
Graham, Franklin, 82
Grand Theft Auto (video game), 30, 38
Grimes, Tom, 14, 34
gun deaths, US vs. Japan, 30

Hald, Gert Martin, 63
Hays, Will, 17
Hays Code, 17–18, 19
Hearst, William Randolph, 15
Heins, Majorie, 29–31, 33
hentai games, 68
Hill, Faith, 67
Holmes, James, 7, 8, 10
Hostel: Part 2 (movie), 75–76
Huesmann, L. Rowell, 44

imitative behavior, described, 12
impulsive behavior, 54
International Society for Research on Aggression, 24–25
Internet, average time on, 21

Japan, 30, 37–38
Jay-Z, 65, **66**
Jenkins, Henry, 12–13
Joker (fictional character), 6, 7
Jones, George, 64
Jones, Lucy, 65
Journal of Sexual Medicine, 63
juvenile offenders, 45–46, **46**

Kelly, Tadhg, 42–43, 51
Kennedy, Helen, 64
Kidman, Nicole, 56, **57**
King, Stephen, 38
Kirsh, Steven J., 15, 17
Kuchera, Ben, 61–62

Lanza, Adam, 6–7, 8, 10, 25, 42
Larry King Live (television program), 47–48
Lieberman, Carole, 62
LimiTV, 79, 81
literature, violence in, 12–13, 70
Los Angeles Times (newspaper), 77, 80

magnetic resonance imaging (MRI), 35
Malamuth, Neil M., 57–58
mass shootings
  mental illness and, 6, 7, 47–48
  public response to, 26, 70–71
  video games and, 7, 28–29, 74
  video games with, 47
McCartney, Jenny, 48
McGraw, Phil, 48
"mean world" syndrome
  described, 12